SAMARKAND AND BUKHARA

TRAVEL TO LANDMARKS

SAMARKAND AND BUKHARA

✸

John Lawton

Photographs by Francesco Venturi

Tauris Parke Books, London

Published by Tauris Parke Books
110 Gloucester Avenue
London NW1 8JA
In association with KEA Publishing Services Ltd, London

Text © 1991 John Lawton
Photographs © 1991 Francesco Venturi/KEA Publishing Services Ltd

TRAVEL TO LANDMARKS
Series Editor: Judy Spours
Editorial Assistant: Elizabeth Harcourt
Designers: Holdsworth Associates
Maps by Andras Bereznay
All Photographs by Francesco Venturi except pages 10, 20, 39, 67.

British Library Cataloguing in Publication Data
    Lawton, John
        Samarkand and Bukhara. – (Travel to landmarks series).
        1. Travel. Uzbekistan
        I. Title II. Series
        915.87

        ISBN 1-85043-178-7

Photosetting by Litho Link Ltd, Welshpool, Powys, UK
Colour separation by Fabbri, Milan, Italy
Printed by Fabbri, Milan, Italy

Frontispiece Muslims used colour in architecture as no other people did, sheathing their buildings with glazed tiles in brilliant hues and rich patterns. This art reached its height under the Timurid dynasty in the cities of Samarkand and Bukhara, where the portal of the Kalyan Mosque exemplifies the two main ways of using tiles: whole to form a larger pattern, or cut to make mosaics. It also illustrates the four main styles of tile decoration: calligraphic, geometric, floral and arabesque.

Contents

Introduction

This Soviet flag caught up on the ornate guttering of a building in Samarkand symbolizes the tangled history of its Uzbek citizens. Swallowed up in the south-easterly advance of the Russian empire during the nineteenth century, the Uzbek people are now seeking to regain their sovereignty from Moscow.

Few landmarks have tantalized the minds of men more than the legendary caravan cities of Central Asia. 'For the lust of knowing what should not be known,' wrote British poet-diplomat James Elroy Flecker, 'we make the Golden Journey . . . to divine *Bukhara* and happy *Samarkand*.' Marlowe, Milton and Keats wrote about these cities too, and so, more recently, did Rudyard Kipling and Oscar Wilde – though none of them had been there.

In fact, so remote behind their barriers of deserts and mountains were Samarkand and Bukhara that, until quite recently, they were visited only rarely by travellers from the West.

One westerner who did reach Central Asia was Marco Polo. He found thirteenth-century Bukhara a 'city most noble and grand,' while Samarkand was 'very large and splendid'. Another, Castilian envoy Don Ruy Gonzales de Clavijo, reported that Samarkand, in the fifteenth century, was 'larger than Seville', and 'among the orchards without are . . . many palaces and pleasure grounds'.

Samarkand and Bukhara at that time were hubs of international trade and cosmopolitan centres of science and art. But by the eighteenth century they had become 'forbidden cities' to all but Muslims. Others who tried to get there either perished *en route* or lost their heads on arrival.

Their inaccessibility only served, however, to fuel men's imaginations. For Keats, recalling the caravans that passed that way from China, Samarkand was 'silken'. While Wilde, throwing botany to the winds, wrote of 'Bukhara where red lilies blow'. Even under Russian control Central Asia was still forbidden to foreigners. One who did make it there – complete with inflatable rubber bath – was the intrepid Victorian traveller, Lord Curzon. He reported that even in decline Bukhara was 'the most interesting city in the world', and Samarkand's Registan its 'noblest square'. Only under Gorbachev has the 'Golden Journey' to Bukhara and Samarkand become simple. From Moscow, Aeroflot, the Soviet national airline, will fly you there in about four hours over the forests, seas and deserts once crossed by Alexander the Great, Genghiz Khan and Timur-the-lame.

These men were drawn there by the lust of conquest – not curiosity. But while the Macedonians and Mongols destroyed them, the Timurids embellished Samarkand and Bukhara until they were the most splendid cities of their time.

When Alexander marched on Marcanda, as Samarkand was then known, it was already one of Asia's largest trading centres. For centuries ancient caravan trails – from Siberia to India, from China to Europe – converged on the verdant oases of Samarkand and Bukhara. Silks and porcelain from the East, amber and furs from the North, gems and spices from the South, and perfumes and ivory from the West, were bartered, bought and sold in their teeming bazaars.

Located at opposite ends of the fertile Zeravshan valley, between the Tien Shan (Heavenly Mountains) in the East and the Kara Kum (Black Sands) desert in the West, the two cities constantly vied for leadership of the region. In the tenth century the Persian Samanids made Bukhara their capital, while in the fourteenth century Timur made Samarkand his. By the eighteenth century Samarkand was subject to Bukhara; following the Soviet revolution their roles were again reversed.

Huge profits derived from the management of international trade made Samarkand and Bukhara centres of luxury – and learning, for ideas too travelled with the merchants and their wares. Some of the world's basic technologies, greatest religions and latest artistic styles were transmitted vast distances via these cities. Many languages were spoken and cultures blended within their walls. The first paper mill west of the Great Wall of China operated in eighth-century Samarkand, while the most influential library in the tenth-century eastern Islamic world was the one in Bukhara.

The commercial and cultural vitality of these two cities lured the finest intellects of the time. The brilliant physician Ibn Sina, known in the West as Avincenna, wrote his celebrated *Canon of Medicine* in Bukhara in the eleventh century. Four hundred years later, the royal astronomer Ulugh Beg, using an enormous sextant set in a hillside overlooking Samarkand, plotted the position of over 1,000 stars.

These cities owed their splendour not only to the accumulation of cultural wealth and profit from trade, but also to the spoils of war. In the fourteenth century, one of the most ferocious warriors the world has ever known, Timur – also known in the West as Tamerlane – conquered all of Asia from the Great Wall of China to the Mediterranean sea. Ordinarily, his taste for battle kept the crippled monarch on the move, but between campaigns he focused his considerable energies on embellishing a capital worthy of his conquests. For this he chose Samarkand, close to his birthplace of Kesh.

Above Samarkand, once a gem of early city planning, now faces acute problems of urbanization. A fifteenth-century visitor reported that 'a traveller who approaches the city sees only the mountainous height of trees, and the houses embowered amongst them remain invisible'. Today, modern buildings soar over the tree-tops and encroach on the majestic lines of the trio of ancient religious colleges flanking Samarkand's famous Registan.

Below Bukhara was once the holiest city of Central Asia, from which, it was said, the light shone up to heaven rather than down. Today, however, the only religious college still functioning in the city is the twin-domed Mir-i-Arab Madrasa, here silhouetted against the night sky together with Bukhara's tallest ancient structure the Kalyan Tower.

Timur embodied the conflicting aspirations of a benevolent builder and marauding murderer; great monuments testified to his beneficence, yet entire populations perished at his hand. From conquered territories in Persia, India and the Middle East, Timur plundered both talented craftsmen and treasures to enhance his capital. What they created was neither Persian, Indian or Arab, although it reflected the influence of all three. Nor was it modelled on the old Samarkand. Instead, these captured architects built a city possessing a new and dazzling Tartar concept.

There were no building materials at Samarkand and so – out of the dust of the surrounding desert, mixed with chopped straw, camel urine and clay from the Zeravshan river – they made mud bricks and with them created swelling domes and towering minarets. These they faced in lovely glazed tiles in every imaginable shade of blue – Timur's favourite colour – until, adorned from top to bottom with glittering tiles Samarkand became the most fabled city of its age. It was this 'blue city' that fired the imagination of Western poets and made men risk their lives to see.

Timur's grandson Ulugh Beg transformed the already spectacular city of Samarkand into one of the cultural and intellectual wonders of the Islamic world. Bukhara under the Timurid dynasty, on the other hand, became one of its holiest cities, boasting a different mosque in which to pray for each day of the year. Elsewhere, it was said, light came down from heaven; from Bukhara it went up.

Despite Timur's victories, his hard-won empire lasted only a few generations. His descendants quarrelled bitterly among themselves – the enlightened Ulugh Beg was murdered by his own son – and were unable to hold together the vast steppe domain that Timur had created.

Weak and disorganized, Central Asia was no longer capable of playing the role of intermediary vital to continued East-West trade. Meanwhile, in 1426, in an effort to expunge long years of foreign influence and resuscitate traditional Chinese values, the Ming Dynasty closed China's borders. After 1,500 years the international trade from which Samarkand and Bukhara had prospered dried up. Economic depression set in, followed by cultural decline. In 1512, Timur's great-great-great-grandson Babur was ejected from Samarkand by the Uzbek Turks, forcing him to flee to India, where he became the first of the Moghal emperors.

The Venetian trader Marco Polo, who crossed Central Asia on his way to China in the thirteenth century, recorded in his famous book *The Travels* that Samarkand was a 'splendid' city and Bukhara was 'most noble'. Mary Evans Picture Library.

Above A graceful ribbed dome covers the mausoleum in Samarkand where Timur lies buried. Lord of Asia from the Tien Shan to the Urals, the Turco-Mongol conqueror made Samarkand his capital in 1370. He embellished it with buildings sheathed in millions of blue-glazed tiles, which even today give the city a distinct character.

Below A cluster of small turquoise domes glistening with intricate Arabic calligraphy mark the Timurid royal cemetery in Samarkand. This spot, known as Shah-i-Zinda (Shrine of the Living King), first became a place of pilgrimage in the eleventh century. Timur rebuilt it as a private necropolis for his family and friends.

Left With four bulbous towers dwarfing a central dome, this strange monument known as Char Minar (Four Minarets) was built in 1807 by a rich Bukhariot merchant as the gateway of a religious college that has since disappeared.

Right This deserted street, leading to the Unfinished Minaret, once throbbed with life – as did the rest of the ancient city of Khiva. The authorities have now evicted most of its inhabitants, and restored it as a lifeless 'town preserve' for tourists.

The Uzbeks, who are still the predominant people of the Zeravshan valley, take their name from Khan Uzbek, the fourteenth-century ruler of the great Turco-Mongol tribal confederation, the Golden Horde, from which they emerged as a distinctive people in the fifteenth century. The Uzbeks continued to rule in Samarkand and Bukhara until the nineteenth century, when their territories were swallowed up by the south-easterly expansion of Russia's czarist empire. Like the rest of Russia, they then fell under the control of the Communists after the 1917 revolution.

Now, however, as the twentieth century draws to a close, the Uzbeks, like other subject nationalities of the USSR, are seeking to regain control of their own destiny. Uzbekistan was the first of the Soviet Union's six Asiatic republics to demand sovereignty from Moscow.

Uzbek leaders claim that, although under Communist rule there have been vast improvements in welfare and education, the Russians have restricted their lives from a religious, political and economic point of view. Moscow, they say, shut down most of their mosques and all but two of their madrasas, or religious colleges. And although there are nearly 20 million Uzbeks in the Soviet Union, only one, Nureddin Muhiddinov, has served on the Politburo during 60 years of Communist rule.

Moreover, the Russians have utilized the resources of Uzbekistan almost as if it were a colony. They designated it the USSR's cotton-growing region and brought vast tracts of 'virgin lands' under cultivation at a high ecological cost. The diversion of rivers to irrigate these lands has resulted in the virtual dessication of the Aral Sea. Once the fourth-largest lake in the world, the Aral has fallen 13.5 m (44 ft) and shrunk to half its original area, leaving a grim desert of chemicals, salt and sand.

Culturally, the Communist's record has been mixed. While they have imposed different Cyrillic alphabets on each of the 11 Turkic nationalities in the USSR, effectively cutting them off from their common literary language, they have poured millions of roubles into restoring their ancient monuments. In some cases, however, they have been over-zealous as in the ejection, for example, of almost the entire population of the 1,000-year-old Central Asian city of Khiva, on the Amu Darya river (ancient Oxus), in order to rebuild it along the lines of a lifeless period 'movie set'.

Above Despite attempts by the Soviets to dilute their Turkic culture, most Uzbek women still prefer to wear in public their traditional Bukhara rainbow silks. This group is visiting the suburban residence of the last Bukhara amirs, who were overthrown by the Soviets in 1920.

Below To climb the steps of Islam Hodja Minaret at Khiva is considered by Muslims to be an act of piety. However, most people do it for the panoramic view that the 50 m (150 ft) tower offers of the Khorezm oasis.

Samarkand, in contrast, faces acute problems of urbanization. Its medieval monuments are at risk from pollution and unbridled urban growth. Traffic roars past the Registan, the rising water table threatens its foundations, and modern buildings encroach on its majestic lines. Timur's citadel and suburban palaces have long since disappeared: felled by earthquakes, vandalized by thieves, or simply blown back into the desert.

Samarkand, too, has lost its role as capital of Uzbekistan to the modern metropolis of Tashkent to the north. But enough remains of Timur's fabled 'blue city' to hint of its grandeur of old. Even in ruins, the great mosque of Bibi Khanum – built to transcend any other in the world – still dwarfs Samarkand today, while recent work on the medieval madrasas flanking three sides of the Registan has restored the ancient plaza to its original splendour. And in the royal cemetery of Shah-i-Zinda, a sea of blues from darkest mauve to palest opalescent, are still held in an incredibly thin glaze, undimmed by six centuries.

In comparison to Samarkand, Bukhara has been treated more kindly by modern development. The modern city has not, as yet, overwhelmed the picturesque old part, where, in the shadow of its ancient monuments, white-bearded men in traditional turbans and striped robes still gather by tree-shaded pools to drink strong black tea with their friends.

In addition, Bukhara has a wider variety of architectural gems from different ages: the tenth-century tomb of the Samanid rulers, striking in its simplicity; the twelfth-century Kalyan tower, with its elaborate brickwork designs; as well as the fourteenth-century tile-faced mosques and madrasas of the Timurid period.

Most of these are now put to secular use. For Bukhara, once famous throughout Asia for its piety and scholarship, is no longer a centre of pilgrimage — or trade. Its main market is now relegated to the suburbs, its 'silks' are factory-made synthetics, and there is no bargaining over the state-fixed price.

Modern travellers who make the Golden Journey to Samarkand and Bukhara may well be disappointed to discover that these cities are no longer as exotic as they imagined. Although this is partly the result of modern development and the passage of time, much of the loss of character is due to decades of Russian repression and sustained attempts by Moscow to break down the religious and cultural unity of the Turkic peoples of Central Asia. However, with nationalism sweeping the Soviet Union these peoples, and especially the Uzbeks whose strong religious and cultural traditions have been difficult to eradicate, are rediscovering their identities. And nowhere is this more apparent than in their renewed respect for their architectural heritage.

1 The Golden Road

For over two thousand years Samarkand and Bukhara were significant actors in world history. They began as oases along the valley of the river Zeravshan, and from about the eighth century BC developed into agricultural centres. As trade routes opened up along the valley, they also became important trading centres, and, being relatively prosperous and strategically placed, they attracted the attention of each successive wave of invaders which, from the sixth century BC, swept through the region. Persians, Greeks, Turks, Arabs and Mongols constantly fought over these cities and the lucrative trade they controlled. And it was from Samarkand, in the fourteenth century, that Timur-the-lame (Tamerlane), declaring that the world was worth only one king, set out to conquer it.

No fully satisfactory explanation has ever been offered for the periodic explosion of nomadic peoples from – or through – Central Asia, but the pattern is clear. The region's sedentary peoples were repeatedly overrun by mounted nomads, and its cities repeatedly razed to the ground and rebuilt with each successive invasion. Each wave of invaders pitched their tents in the ruins of the cities and settled down, adopting the civilized ways of those they had conquered. And, having become soft themselves, they submitted in turn to a new wave of hardy invaders.

The region, in fact, has acted as a dynamo, generating population movements that have affected Europe and Asia since the beginning of recorded history. From the Eurasian steppes came the Huns, Turks and Mongols. The last great wave of invasion stemming from Central Asia occurred in the late fourteenth century, when Timur and his Turco-Mongol hordes devastated western Asia and the Middle East. And finally, in the early sixteenth century, the Uzbeks overwhelmed the dynasty Timur had created, and made his legendary 'blue' capital, Samarkand, and Bukhara their own. Descended from some of the world's most powerful peoples – the fierce mounted bowmen of Attila, Bumin, Genghiz Khan and Timur – the Uzbeks have since then occupied an area between the Amu Darya and Syr Darya rivers – modern Uzbekistan.

Much of the region's turbulent history stemmed from competition for control of the lucrative trade route, known as the Golden Road, which crossed it, and for the fortress towns and agricultural centres such as Samarkand, Bukhara and Khiva, that had developed along it.

While the Arabs stayed in Central Asia for only two centuries, they left an indelible imprint – bestowing on its people the Muslim religion. Practised there since the ninth century, Islam is still – despite Soviet attempts to eradicate it – Central Asia's only religion, and a unifying force among its people. Here a believer prays at Hazrati Imam Mosque at Shahrisabz.

The Golden Road linked Samarkand and Bukhara with the metropoles of Mesopotamia, and got its name, according to Flecker, because it was 'a desert path as yellow as the bright sea-shore'. Less poetic, but more probable, is that it was so-called because of the huge profits made from the merchandise that flowed along it: silk, porcelain and lacquer-ware from China, gems and spices from India, furs from Siberia, incense from Arabia, ivory from Africa, amber from the Baltic, glass-ware from Syria, and gold and silver from Rome.

The Golden Road was one of the busiest of the Silk Roads – the network of trade routes which linked East and West for 1500 years, and which were a major conduit for technological innovation and religious change. Highways that helped shape history, the Silk Roads were the line of march of Alexander the Great, Genghis Khan and Timur. But above all they were great channels of communication. To the West, via the Silk Roads, were transmitted the Chinese inventions of printing and paper-making, while eastwards travelled viticulture. And two of the world's most widespread religions, Buddhism and Islam, were spread by monks in saffron robes and pious Arab merchants who travelled along them. Craftsmen, scholars, entertainers and official emissaries from far lands also travelled the Silk Roads, which inevitably formed a cultural causeway carrying new philosophies, new fashions, new artistic styles over vast distances.

Alexander the Great siezed Samarkand and Bukhara in 326 BC on his headlong march across Central Asia to win the largest empire the world had yet known. It was at Samarkand that Alexander, in a druken rage, slew his loyal general Cleitus, to whom he owed his life. Mary Evans Picture Library.

At their zenith, in AD 200, the Silk Roads and their western connections through the Roman road system constituted the longest overland trade route on earth: a travelling distance of some 12,800 km (8000 miles) from Cadiz on the Atlantic coast to Shanghai on the Pacific Ocean. And from the main routes subsidiary ones branched out into other networks covering Russia, India and the Middle East. And linking them all, across Central Asia, was the Golden Road.

The Legacy of Alexander the Great

The Persian Achaemendis, including Cyrus the Great, Xerxes and three rulers all named Darius, were the first to establish an empire that extended over parts of Central Asia. This empire dates back to 599 BC and, according to inscriptions at Behistun, it included Sogdiana – a desert kingdom between the Amu Darya and Syr Darya rivers.

Between 330 and 327 BC, Alexander the Great, King of Macedonia, overthrew the Achaemendis as he conquered most of the land from the

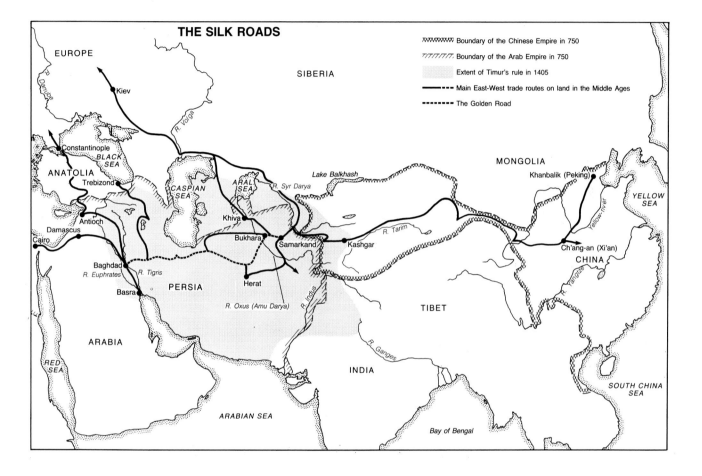

THE SILK ROADS

Boundary of the Chinese Empire in 750
Boundary of the Arab Empire in 750
Extent of Timur's rule in 1405
Main East-West trade routes on land in the Middle Ages
The Golden Road

EUROPE

SIBERIA

MONGOLIA

Kiev

R. Danube

R. Volga

Constantinople

BLACK SEA

ANATOLIA

Trebizond

CASPIAN SEA

ARAL SEA

R. Syr Darya

Lake Balkhash

Khanbalik (Peking)

YELLOW SEA

Antioch

Khiva

Damascus

Cairo

Bukhara

Samarkand

Kashgar

R. Tarim

Yellow river

Ch'ang-an (Xi'an)

CHINA

Baghdad

R. Euphrates

R. Tigris

PERSIA

Herat

R. Oxus (Amu Darya)

R. Indus

R. Yangtze

Basra

ARABIA

R. Ganges

TIBET

RED SEA

INDIA

SOUTH CHINA SEA

ARABIAN SEA

Bay of Bengal

Mediterranean to the Indus river valley of India. Samarkand and Bukhara, which by then had developed into strongly fortified trading centres, fell in 328 BC after pitched battles.

The Sogdians, however, continued to wage guerilla war against the Macedonians, and, in what official Soviet history calls 'one of the earliest peoples' liberation movements,' inflicted the worst defeat ever suffered by Alexander's forces. While Alexander was away fighting the Scythians, the Sogdians beseiged Samarkand, and then ambushed and massacred the Macedonian force sent to relieve it.

To cope with the hit-and-run tactics of the widely scattered rebel forces, Alexander abandoned his traditional phalanx formation and divided his army into five very mobile columns. These swept through Sogdiana, storming fortified positions and systematically devastating the Zeravshan valley in order to prevent the Sogdians returning to Samarkand.

However, the war in Sogdiana was still not over. Many rebels, including the Baron Oxyartes of Bactria, took refuge in a rocky fortress in the east of the country known as the 'Sogdian Rock.' The Rock was sheer on all sides, and the Sogdians claimed Alexander would need 'winged Soldiers' to capture it. But 300 Macedonians, using linen ropes and iron tent-pegs as pitons, scaled the Rock during the night and forced the astounded Oxyartes to make peace.

According to Alexander's biographer Arrian, when Alexander saw Oxyartes' daughter Roxane, he 'fell in love with her at sight', and the marriage was soon solemnized, according to local custom, by the cutting of a loaf of bread. Less romantic, but more probable, is that it was a political match aimed at finally securing the allegiance of the troublesome Sogdians.

When Alexander died, struck down by fever at the age of 32, only two years after marrying Roxane, his empire was divided among his generals. One of them, Seleucus, won control of the eastern part and founded the Seleucid dynasty. However, the sheer size of these Greco-Asiatic domains made them difficult to rule. In the more remote areas, particularly in Central Asia, native aristocrats took matters into their own hands, appointing their own governors and refusing to acknowledge the authority of the Seleucid king.

By the middle of the third century BC, the governor of Bactria, which included Sogdiana, had proclaimed independence from Seleucia, and an

Iranian chieftain had staged a successful revolt in Parthia. Within a century, the Parthians had overthrown the Seleucides, blocked the eastward advance of the Romans, and established themselves as middlemen in the rich East-West trade.

In the second century AD Parthian power began to wane. Part of the resulting power vacuum in Central Asia was filled by the Kushans, a semi-nomadic people who controlled the trade routes through the Pamirs and the caravan centres of Samarkand and Bukhara. The third-century Sassanian revolution in Iran brought dynamic new leadership to the region. By the fourth century, the Sassanians had wrested control of Central Asia from the Kushans, and reimposed a central authority over the trade routes.

However, by the middle of the sixth century new disturbances broke out on the steppes, and once again central authority over the trade routes was lacking. Trade continued, however, partly as a result of the activities of city-dwelling minorities, such as the Sogdians of Samarkand, whose communities provided secure and settled conditions for the exchange of goods.

The Growth of the Islamic Empire

At this stage a new group of steppe nomads suddenly appeared: the Turks. Their origins, like those of nearly all Central Asian peoples, are shrouded in mystery and legend. The story favoured by the Turks themselves centres around the mythical union of a she-wolf and a youth – the sole survivor of the tribal massacre – which produced ten boys. One of these, A-Shin-na, founded the line which in turn, several generations later, gave rise to the Turks (the word Turk means 'forceful' or 'strong').

The rise of the world's first Turkic empire, typically for the steppelands, revolved around a single charismatic personality – Bumin. The Turk's homeland was in the Altai mountain range in present-day Mongolia, where they were originally a subject people of the Juan-Juan, whom they served as blacksmiths and ironworkers. Bumin challenged the Juan-Juan overlordship by requesting a Juan-Juan princess in marriage. When the request was refused, the Turks, allied with the forces of the Western Wei, destroyed the Juan-Juan state, in 552. They then subjugated their nomadic neighbours to become uncontested masters of the Mongolian steppe.

Above International trading centres for 1500 years, Bukhara's bazaars were once the richest in Central Asia. The most important ones were located near the city's ll gates which served the caravan trails that crossed there, or near places of worship, where people always gathered. This domed bazaar, which is still in use today, adjoins Bukhara's main religious complex, Poi Kalyan, in the background.

Below Since the demise of the Silk Roads, due to the opening of sea routes between Europe and the Far East in the late fifteenth century, Central Asia no longer trades in exotic goods or plays host to merchants from far lands. Its markets, however, remain colourful, even though, like this one at Shahrisabz, its traders and produce are local.

Moving westwards, the Turks conquered Central Asia and reached the Volga; in the east their power extended to the Yellow River. It was the first time so great an expanse of Asia had come under the control of a single ethnic group. As the Turks fanned out across the steppe, tribal divisions among them became more pronounced, and several Turkish tribes, including the Kirgiz, Qarluq and Uygur, established their own kingdoms.

Then, like a great swordthrust from the west, came the Arabs, under the banner of Islam. The swiftness of their early conquests were astonishing; scarcely two decades after the death of the Muslim prophet Muhammad, in 623, the entire Near East had fallen to the Arabs. It was some time, however, before they turned their attention to Central Asia and the cities of Samarkand and Bukhara – once again under the influence of the Sogdians, who had come to an uneasy alliance with the Turks.

Arab soldiers initially crossed the Amu Darya in 654, but it was not until 705, when Qutaiba ibn Muslim became the governor of Khorasan, that the Arabs achieved real success in Central Asia. Even then they had their problems. One of these was the beautiful Princess Khatum, queen-regent of Bukhara during the minority of her son. Khatum it is said fled to Samarkand before the Arab armies, shedding a slipper worth 200,000 *direms* – the most valuable slipper of all time. But she was soon back, leading the people in revolt and re-establishing herself in Bukhara. It was to take three years – from 706 to 709 – and four campaigns before the Bukhariots were finally subdued.

Samarkand too changed hands on several occasions, falling finally to Qutaiba in 711. Legend relates that on the arrival of his forces outside Samarkand, the inhabitants shouted from the walls that they were wasting their time. 'We have found it written', they said, 'that our city can only be captured by a man named "Camel-saddle".' Being ignorant of Arabic they did not know that 'Qutaiba' meant exactly that.

By the middle of the eighth century most of Central Asia had been incorporated into the Islamic realm. But this conquest put the Arabs on a collision course with China, which was also in the midst of a period of vigorous expansion.

The two medieval superpowers met for the first and only time in 751, at Talas near Dzhambul in present-day Kazakstan, in a battle to determine which of the two civilizations – Muslim or Chinese – would

One of the oldest surviving
mosques in Central Asia is the
twelfth-century Magok-i-Attari
Mosque in Bukhara, noted for
the complex geometric patterns
executed in carved ceramic on its
portal.

Besides Islam, the Arabs bequeathed to Central Asia the Arabic script, which was widely used there for 1300 years both for writing and architectural decoration – as in this calligraphic inscription in Samarkand's Timurid royal cemetery, Shah-i-Zinda. Fifty years ago, however, the Soviet government imposed Cyrillic alphabets on its Muslim nationalities.

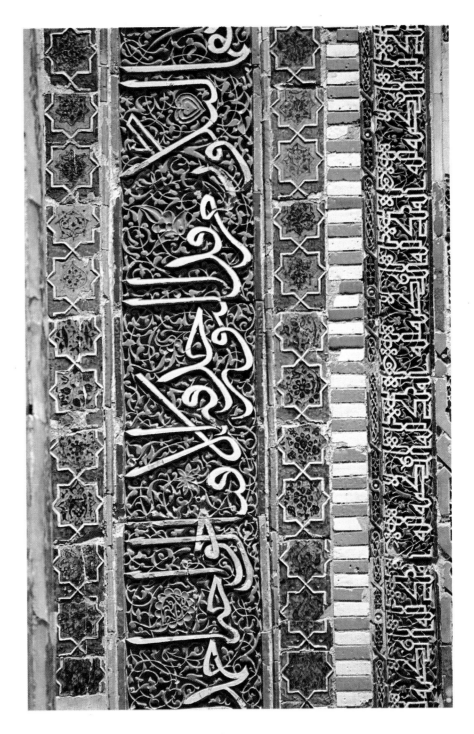

dominate Central Asia. Neither of these empires were actually planning war – and none would have occurred then had the unexpected not happened. A purely local quarrel between the two petty kingdoms of Ferghana and Chach caused Ferghana to seek military assistance from China, and Chach to appeal for help to the Arabs. The clash of the colossi at Talas lasted five days, with the two titans attacking, retreating, reforming and attacking again inconclusively. The battle was eventually decided by a third force – the mounted bowmen of the Qarluq Turks.

Chinese chronicles say the Turks treacherously changed sides in the midst of the action, attacking them from the rear. Arab historians, on the other hand, claim that the Turks were allied with them all along and the attack from behind was part of a carefully pre-arranged battle plan. Whatever the truth of the matter, the Chinese army broke and fled, never to return to Central Asia. The Arabs prudently refrained from pursuit, and that was the end of their territorial expansion too.

But the battle of Talas was not only a political and military landmark. It had important technological consequences, too. Chinese prisoners captured at Talas and taken to Samarkand taught the Arabs how to make paper – a process they in turn transmitted to the West.

Although the Arabs stayed in Central Asia for only two centuries, they left an indelible imprint on the region south of the Aral Sea, bestowing upon it the Muslim religion and Arabic script – both of which have been practised and used there almost ever since.

Each civilization that embraced Islam also adopted non-representational art and calligraphic decoration, which grew out of the religion's prohibition of human images for worship. But although the Arabs, through their construction and decoration of mosques and madrasas, also set an architectural tradition followed in Central Asia for centuries, little actual physical evidence of their – or earlier invaders' – presence remains. This is partly because of the region's turbulent history – Samarkand and Bukhara were repeatedly razed to the ground; its lack of long-lasting construction material, such as stone; the preference of its nomadic invaders for tents, rather than brick walls; and little archeological investigation of the region.

In fact, the earliest relatively intact architectural remains of the Zeravshan valley is the tenth-century mud brick mausoleum of the Samanids at Bukhara, which survived because it was completely buried

Further Arab influence on Central Asian architecture is evident in this deeply recessed 'stalactite' archway at Bukhara's Abd al-Aziz Madrasa – typical of the Middle East.

By the beginning of the twentieth-century there were some 26,000 mosques in Central Asia. This, the Hazrati Hizr Mosque in Samarkand, was built in the nineteenth century and restored in 1913. Mosque building was stopped by the Communists after the 1917 revolution, and all but 400 of the mosques in the region were shut down between 1928 and 1938.

and was discovered by chance. The Samanids emerged in the ninth century as the first independent Muslim state in Central Asia. Its capital was Bukhara, which under Samanid rule became the showplace of Central Asia, and from its strategic position on the Golden Road became one of the great commercial centres of the Muslim world.

By the tenth century Islam had become the predominant religion in Central Asia replacing Buddhism, Manicheism and Zoroastrianism, which had virtually ceased to exist. However, although they adopted Islam, the Turks stubbornly preserved their own traditions and culture. Turkish became the majority language of Central Asia, which became known as Turkestan.

Commerce flourished along the Golden Road, Samarkand and Bukhara became rich and grew into large metropolises, and Central Asia became one of the world's most verdant and influential centres of culture. At Bukhara, Ibn Sina (Avincenna), born in 980 and for centuries considered the 'prince of all learning', wrote *The Canon of Medicine*, a systematic encyclopaedia based on the achievements of Greek and Arab physicians, which, translated into Latin, was used as a textbook in medieval Europe.

At Khiva, meanwhile, al-Biruni, born in 973, searched in every branch of human knowledge, anticipating the principles of modern geology, laying the foundation for astronomy, investigating the relative speeds of sound and light; and – 600 years before Galileo – he discussed the possibility of the earth's rotation around its own axis.

In the final year of the tenth century, the Samanid dynasty was overthrown by the Karahanid Turks, who made Samarkand their capital and ruled over most of the region until the middle of the twelfth century, when they in turn were displaced by the Kara-Kitais, nomads of Chinese culture and probably Mongolian origin. In the eleventh century a new power had arisen in Central Asia – the Seljuq Turks. They swept west into present-day Iran, Iraq, Syria and finally Turkey – to which they gave their name. Originally the Seljuq dominions included the oasis of Khiva, or Khorezm, along the Amu Darya river southwest of the Aral Sea. But the Khorezmshahs appointed by the Seljuq sultan to govern there soon tired of being vassals and, in 1077, established an independent state of their own, with their capital at Urgench, close to present-day Khiva. By the beginning of the thirteenth century, having brought both Bukhara and Samarkand under their

The first independent Muslim state in Central Asia was that of the Persian Samandis. They made their capital at Bukhara, and built a mausoleum for their dynasty there that is regarded as one of the finest achievements of early medieval architecture. By laying the mud bricks with which it was built at different angles tenth-century craftsmen covered the mausoleum with intricate geometric patterns.

control, the Khorezmshahs had made themselves the paramount power in Central Asia.

Genghiz Khan

It was into this tangled world of overlapping dynasties and ever-shifting spheres of influence that Temujin, later known as Genghiz Khan, was born in Mongolia. In legend the offspring of a deer and a wolf, and in reality the son of a Mongol chieftain, Genghiz Khan began his career by subduing the tribes he blamed for his father's murder. By 1206 he had welded all the tribes of Mongolia into a single confederacy and forged their cavalry into a formidable war machine.

It was not long before trouble arose between the Mongols and their western neighbours the Khorezmshahs. In 1218 a caravan of 450 merchants *en route* from Mongolia were murdered and their goods stolen by the Khorezmian governor of Otrar. And when Genghiz Khan sent a protest to the Khorezmshahs, his envoy too was murdered.

This incident changed the face of Central Asia, and indeed the world, for it triggered the most devastating invasion of steppe nomads in history. Genghiz Khan punished this interference with free trade – an essential goal of Mongol policy – by unleashing 200,000 men, first against Otrar, then against Urgench, Bukhara and Samarkand.

Soon all of Central Asia and Persia had felt the wrath of the Mongols as they pursued the fleeing shah of Khorezm, Muhammad, as far as the Caspian Sea. A local historian who managed to escape from Bukhara summed up the Mongol onslaught in one line: 'Amadand, u kandang, u sukhtand, u kushtand, u burdand, u raftand' (They came, they uprooted, they burned, they slew, they despoiled, they departed).

Other chroniclers say the Bukhariots bravely resisted the Mongol hordes, and it was only when the governor 'seeing himself and Friends overwhelm'd with Pots thrown in full of Naphta and Fire, and the Gates of the Castle in Flames, surrender'd'.

Samarkand, according to the same sources, although defended by 100,000 troops and having 'more fortifications than Bukhara . . . 12 Gates made of Iron, and at every two Leagues a fort', gave up without much of a fight. Perhaps because of this, the Mongols allowed most of the inhabitants to live on in what remained of the city after they ritually sacked and looted it.

That the destruction of Samarkand was far from total is attested to

The ruined piers of the great central arch of the entrance portal is all that remains of the palace that Timur built at Shahrisabz, which he originally intended as his capital. At least 50 m (165 ft) high, and with a span of about 22 m (74 ft), it was one of the largest man-made archways of its time.

Above When he died in 1405, leading his army against China, Timur was carried back to Samarkand and buried in the mausoleum he had built for his grandson, Muhammad Sultan. From then on, it became the Timurid dynasty sepulchre, known as Gur-i-Amir – the Ruler's Tomb.

Below Although Timur's palace at Shahrisabz was known as Akserai, the White Palace, its portal was covered in blue and gold tiles, which – even in decay – still retain their lustre.

by the Arab traveller Ibn Battuta, who passed that way in 1333. Even though, he reported, it now had no walls or gates and most of its palaces were in ruins, it was still, he said: 'one of the largest and most perfectly beautiful cities in the world . . . built on the bank of a river where the inhabitants promenade after afternoon prayer'.

Bukhara, however, Ibn Battuta found: 'destroyed by the accursed Tinkiz (Genghiz) . . . and all but a few of its mosques, academies and bazaars lying in ruins.' While its inhabitants, once renowned for their piety and enlightenment, were now: 'looked down upon . . . because of their fanaticism and falsehood.'

Genghiz Khan's sons conquered China, Eastern Europe and the Middle East. At its zenith their empire was one of the largest the world has ever known – stretching from the Pacific to the Danube and from Burma to Siberia. The Mongols ruled this massive empire by force, imposing within its borders a respect for law that was absolute. French historian Louis Boulnois quotes a saying that 'a girl could walk across (the Mongolian empire) from one end to the other bearing a golden dish on her head without being molested.' And although history remembers them as marauders, it was during this so-called 'Mongol Peace' in Central Asia that European merchants – among them Marco Polo – were safely able to traverse the normally unruly steppes, establishing direct contact between China and the West for the very first time.

Before he died, Genghiz Khan divided his dominions between his four sons. Turkestan, including Samarkand and Bukhara, went to his second son, Chaghatai, whose descendants ruled there for almost a century. But unlike their cousins of the Golden Horde in the north, Yuan dynasty in the east, and Il-Khans in the west, the Chaghatai Khans were unremarkable rulers. During their reign the cities of Central Asia fell into decay, and by the middle of the fourteenth century their dynasty had disintegrated.

The Age of Timur-the-lame

The dream of Asian empire, however, was not dead. A final glorious chapter in the history of Turkestan was written in the late fourteenth and early fifteenth centuries by the Timurid dynasty. During this time, literature and art revived, trade flourished, and the phoenix-like cities of Samarkand and Bukhara rose again to even greater prominence.

Timur, the dynasty's founder, was born in Kesh, just south of

The vivid mosaic panels, exquisitely embossed tiles and carved ceramic columns of Shah-i-Zinda, the Timurid royal cemetery in Samarkand, are considered the finest glazed decor in all of Central Asia.

Samarkand, in 1336, the son of a Turco-Mongol chieftain. A wound in the leg, inflicted in a local rebellion, gave him the name Timur-the-lame. A born leader with a genius for strategy – and an outstanding chess player – Timur was only 21 when, modelling himself on Genghiz Khan, he set out to conquer the world.

In a succession of military campaigns lasting half a century, Timur carved out an empire stretching from the Indus River valley to the Black Sea. Brutal slaughters often followed his victories, and grisly pyramids of enemy skulls commemorated the passage of his troops. By 1370 Timur was undisputed leader of Turkestan, and built an impregnable citadel at Samarkand. In 1380 he defeated the Il-Khans to become master of Persia, and in three campaigns against the Golden Horde, overwhelmed them also. In 1398 Timur conducted a devastating campaign against India, and the following year invaded Georgia. In 1401 he stormed Baghdad and Damascus, breaking the power of the Mamelukes in Mesopotamia, and in 1402 defeated the Turkish Ottomans at Ankara, before sacking the Christian stronghold of Smyrna (Izmir) on the Aegean Sea. Had he not died of pneumonia in 1405 as he was leading his armies against China, Timur may even have conquered that too.

'If I were alive', says a grim inscription in an ante-room of Timur's tomb in Samarkand, 'people would not be glad'. Possibly: after his conquest of Baghdad, Timur's troops – portrayed in this Persian-style miniature painting – paraded before him holding the severed heads of their enemies. These were later used to build a tomb. By permission of the British Library.

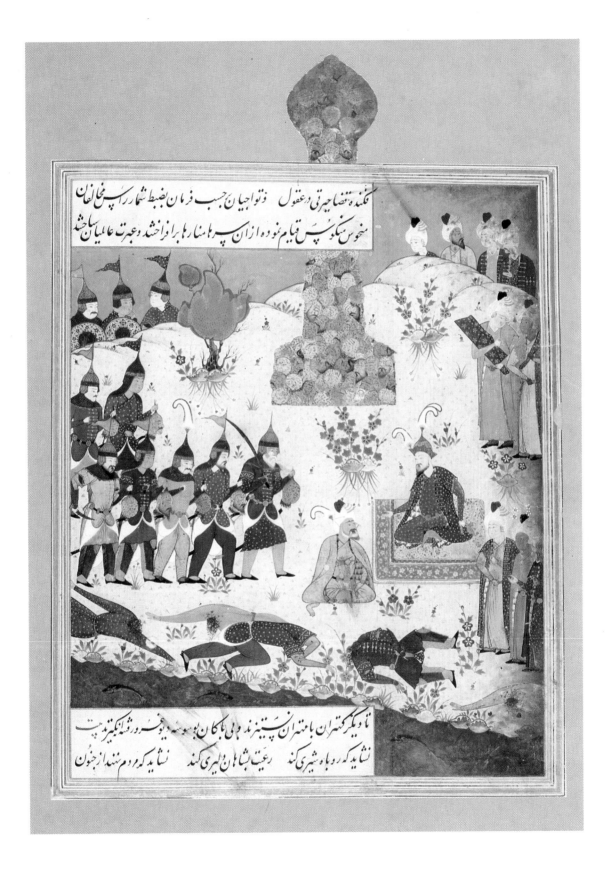

2   Happy Samarkand

Set in a vast desert, the life of Samarkand has always depended on the Zeravshan river flowing from the snows and glaciers of the Heavenly Mountains 320 km (200 miles) to the east. From prehistoric times, settled groups of people have lived in the Zeravshan valley, clustering around the hillside streams, and later, with the development of irrigation, following them down into the plains. Archaeological studies have revealed four neolithic sites located on hillside terraces 27 km (17 miles) southwest of Samarkand. And always, the harsher nomad hordes from the surrounding deserts and northern steppes have overwhelmed them and become in turn their settlers.

Tradition ascribes the foundation of Samarkand, in the fifth century BC, to Afrasiyab, a semi-mythical Sogdian king. It emerges from legend into history in manuscripts describing the fourth century BC conquests of Alexander the Great. It was at Samarkand, or Marcanda as it was then known, that his forces suffered one of their few defeats.

Samarkand originally stood on a 290-hectare (714-acre) triangle of high ground, fringed by deep gullies, in the north eastern suburbs of the present city. Today, apart from archaeologists and shepherds with their flocks, this extensive grass-covered site – known as Afrasiyab – is abandoned: a cluster of lifeless hillocks with nothing to suggest that ancient civilizations once flourished there.

The hills of Afrasiyab, however, hide the ruins of a unique Central Asian city, which already in the time of Alexander was an unusually large fortified settlement with a substantial population, developed crafts, commerce and culture. It had a citadel and an external defence wall which the Macedonian manuscripts estimated at 70 stadia (some 14 km, or about 9 miles). Archaeologists have discovered remnants of these fortifications, and a section 80 m long and 13 m high (262 ft long and 43 ft high) has been cleared for closer inspection. At the foot of what they believe to be the citadel, archaeologists have also unearthed traces of palaces, temples, market-places and a network of streets and canals.

Afrasiyab was first abandoned during the eighth-century Arab conquests, when the city was raised by Qutaiba ibn Muslim. When Samarkand revived, Afrasiyab became an artisans' quarter.

Also on the hills of Afrasiyab, archaeologists have discovered the ruins of a large mosque where, they believe, a group of defenders made

Held in an incredibly thin glaze, the colours of these carved tiles adorning the mortuary chapels of Timur's relatives and friends at Shah-i-Zinda remain as radiant as the day they were made – a triumph for fourteenth and fifteenth-century Central Asian ceramists.

a last stand against the hordes of Genghiz Khan. They found there
fragments of mail and armour, and, on a wall blackened by fire, a
prayer scratched with a knife by a wounded warrior. Since the Mongols
sacked Samarkand in 1220, Afrasiyab has remained abandoned. But a
small modern museum built on the edge of the ancient site exhibits
some reminders of its inhabited days: terracotta figurines and pottery,
jewelry and coins, and a copy of a magnificent but much-damaged
mural of processional scenes, which adorned the walls of a seventh-
century dwelling. The original is in the Hermitage Museum in
Leningrad.

Timur's Samarkand

Timur built his medieval city just south of ancient Samarkand. He
surrounded it, according to one account, with a massive wall which had
six gates and was about 7 km (4½ miles) long. A citadel was built in the
western section of the city, protected on all sides by deep ravines. Inside
the citadel stood the Kok-Saray, or Blue Palace, Timur's official
residence and treasury. Next to Kok-Saray were government offices and
an armoury, where a thousand armourers are said to have worked
unceasingly, making bows and arrows, armour and helmets, spears and
swords, for Timur's unrelenting campaigns.

Timur's ferocity against his enemies was rivalled only by his
munificence towards his capital. Laying waste to other capitals, he
lavished their plundered treasures and talent on his own, and, between
campaigns, personally supervised the building of its monuments and
the welfare of its people. 'Everywhere there was security, tranquility,
leisure and comfort,' wrote Don Ruy Gonzales de Clavijo, the
ambassador of King Henry III of Castile and Leon to Timur's court in
the final months of his reign. 'Grain was cheap, needs were satisfied;
there was equality of fortune, justice of the Amir (Timur), health of
body, fair weather, ceasing of enmity, attainment of desire and the
company of the beloved.' Little wonder Flecker called it 'happy
Samarkand'.

This munificence was not, however, motivated purely by selflessness
on Timur's part. As Lord of Asia he needed an imposing capital to
reflect his power, and, despite his nomadic roots, Timur enjoyed the
pleasures of civilization. After each victorious campaign, he carried off
to Samarkand the master craftsmen of the nation he had conquered:

SAMARKAND

Site of Ulugh Beg's Observatory

Afrasiyab

Bibi Khanum Mosque

Hazrati Shah-i-Zinda Shrine

Ploshchad Lenina

Tilikar Madrasa

Shirdar Madrasa

Ulugh Beg Madrasa

Ploshchad Registan

Gur-i-Amir Mausoleum

Ulitsa Akademika Abdullayeva
Ulitsa Tashkentskaya
Ulitsa Titova
Ulitsa
Ulitsa
Kairuanskaya
Dagbitskaya
Ulitsa Frunze
Kommunisticheskaya
Ulitsa
Uzbekistanskaya
Ahunbabayeva
Gorkovo
Ulitsa Maxima
Bulvar
Registanskaya
Umarova
Ulitsa
Suzangaranskaya
Andizhanskaya
Ulitsa
Ulitsa
Penjikentskaya
Ulitsa
Ulitsa
Jurakulova
Ulitsa
Kavarzar
Tashkentskaya

Left In medieval Central Asia, the practice of covering buildings with coloured tiles became more than mere decoration. As is illustrated by the contrasting colours and patterns of the wall, dome and stepped drum of the Tilakari Mosque in Samarkand, it was consciously used to emphasize and enhance architectural elements.

Right Considered from an architectural point of view to be Central Asia's noblest square, Samarkand's Registan has been restored to its former glory. Of the trio of monumental religious colleges flanking the square, the fifteenth-century Ulugh Beg Madrasa, on the left of the picture, is the oldest and most beautiful. In the centre of the picture is the Tilakar Madrasa, and on the right, the Shirdar Madrasa – both built 200 years later.

Above From prehistoric times, farmers clustered around the hillside streams of the Zeravshan Valley. And although with the advent of irrigation most moved down to the plains, some still live on the hillsides today. Their lifestyle has changed little with the passage of time. Here, a young woman at Hazrati Doud bakes bread in a mud-brick oven.

Right It is different to grasp the enormity of the façades of the buildings surrounding the Registan without comparisons for scale. These people passing in front of one of the square's corner columns are only half the height of its base alone.

Although built in imitation of the Ulugh Beg Madrasa which it faces across the Registan, the seventeenth-century Shirdar, or Lion-bearing, Madrasa lacks the purity and harmony of style and decoration of its fifteenth-century model. It takes its name from the crude representation of the 'lion' (in close up it resembles a tiger) in the rays of the rising sun, which surmounts the giant central archway of its façade *(left)*.

sculptors and stucco-workers from Azerbaijan and Delhi, tile and mosaic-workers from Shiraz and Isfahan, silk-weavers and ceramists from Damascus, and stonemasons and silversmiths from Turkey. And while they went to work embellishing his capital, Timur, according to de Clavijo, 'loosed for men the reins of indulgence and pleasure', and hosted weeks of feasting on the banks of the river Zeravshan nearby.

Together with the architects of Turkestan, Timur's captured craftsmen constituted one of the most powerful creative forces ever gathered in one place. The pool of great artistic and constructional tradition created by their presence, combined with the high level of mathematical science – the basis of medieval architecture – in Samarkand at that time, brought about a building renaissance in Central Asia.

Little is known about the men who laboured in great haste – Timur was always in a hurry – with few building materials but mud, to create, in Marlowe's words, a city:

> Famous through the furthiest continents . . .
> Whose shining turrets shall dismay the heavens,
> And cast the fame of Ilion's tower to hell.

However, the most magnificent buildings in Samarkand today are theirs. And the influence of their architectural style – both in concept and decoration – is apparent from Delhi to Istanbul.

Muslims in general used colour in architecture as no other people have done, clothing their buildings both inside and out with brilliant hues and rich patterns in polished brickwork, faience (decorated porcelain and pottery) mosaic and glazed tiles. But the extraordinary flourishing of the art of ceramic revetment (the covering or facing of a wall) under the Timurids holds a distinct place in architectural history. For during the Timurid period the covering of buildings with coloured materials became more than a mere decoration; it was consciously used to underline the architectural elements.

There are two ways of using tiles in architectural decoration: in mosaics, where pieces of different coloured tiles are cut into smaller pieces to create an overall pattern; and as whole tiles, each coloured and patterned so that in combination they form a larger design. And there are four main styles of tile decoration: calligraphic, geometric, floral, and arabesque in which stylized plant stems twinning upon each other form a beautiful fretted pattern. The style of architecture consisted of a dome supported by a conical base, which sat on a drum, which in turn sat on the building. Each element in this construction was faced with a different style of decoration in order to emphasize and enhance them.

Timur's captured architects used glazed brick, faience mosaic and tiles to embellish the tall minarets, giant domes and stout portals of the mosques, madrasas and mausoleums they built at Samarkand. The dominant colours they used were turquoise and celestial blues – Timur's favourites; and their lustre – undimmed by six centuries of sun, wind and rain – is a triumph for fourteenth- and fifteenth-century Central Asian ceramists.

Timur's builders did not confine themselves to monumental architecture. On the outskirts of Samarkand they laid out a series of royal gardens in which they built pavilions and small palaces, and where Timur, a restless nomad, would pitch his silken tents – moving from one garden to another every few days.

It was in one of these royal retreats – Bagh-i-digusha or Garden of the Heart's Delight – that the Castilian envoy Don de Clavijo, to whom we owe the most detailed and colourful account of Samarkand, first met Timur.

'We found Timur seated under a portal before a most beautiful palace,' relates de Clavijo. 'He was lounging against some pillows upon a raised dais before which there was a fountain where red apples floated. He was dressed in a cloak of plain silk, and he wore a tall white hat on the crown of which was displayed a balas ruby, and was further ornamented with pearls and precious stones.' Of the garden where the audience took place, de Clavijo wrote:

> The parterres were laid out with perfect symmetry in alleys, square beds, and little wildernesses of divers figures. Sycamore trees were planted on the borders of the alleys, and the compartments on all sides filled with different sorts of fruit trees, and others which bore only flowers. At each of the four corners of the garden a lofty pavilion was erected, covered with porcelain and having very delicate shadowing, ranged with admirable art and skill.

In the middle of the garden, de Clavijo said, stood a three-storey palace 'adorned with all the beauties which could charm the eyes of men.' Its ceilings were decorated with floral-patterned faience mosaic, its walls lined with porcelain, and it was surrounded by a colonnade of marble. The palace was dedicated to one of Timur's wives, Tukel Khanum, and was said to have been built in only a few weeks by craftsmen working by torchlight throughout the night.

The abilities of Timur's builders is further attested to by another visitor to Samarkand, Sharak al-Din Ali Yazdi. Writing about the palace of Bagh-i-shimal, the Garden of the North, designed by architects from Damascus, he said:

> And what is most remarkable about these able men is that with stones of different colours they made on the walls and floors designs which marquetry workers had made only with ebony and ivory . . . Afterwards workmen from Persia and Iraq decorated the outside of the walls with faience from Kashan.

De Clavijo records that besides Arabs and Persians, Samarkand's population included 'Turks and Moors of diverse sects, with Christians who were Greeks and Armenians,' and totalled about 150,000.

Of the city itself, de Clavijo relates:

> Samarkand stands in a plain and is surrounded by a rampart of earth with a very deep ditch. Lying outside the wall are great numbers of houses, which form extensive suburbs. All round the city are orchards and vineyards, in between which are streets and open squares, all densely populated. Thus it is that the population outwith the city is more numerous that the population within the walls.
>
> Round and about the great men of the government also have their estates and country houses, each standing within its orchards; and so numerous are there gardens and vineyards surrounding Samarkand that a traveller who approaches that city sees only a great mountainous height of trees and the houses embowered among them remain invisible.
>
> Beyond the suburbs of Samarkand stretch the great plains . . . with open fields through which the river flows, being diverted into many water courses, between which are melon beds and cotton growing lands.

In these plains were many villages, which, to underscore the superiority of his capital over others, Timur named after such cities as

Above Although Uzbek embellishment of domes and minarets with faience mosaic and glazed tile – exemplified here at Shirdar Madrasa – was more elaborate than Timurid ceramic, it is somewhat inferior in artistic terms.

Below Typical of Muslim architecture, the monumental portal of Tilakari Madrasa – some 30 m (100 ft) in height – served to keep private the interior of the building while announcing its presence by an impressive façade.

Misr (Cairo), Dimishk (Damascus), Baghdad and Shiraz. 'The richness and abundance of this great capital,' wrote de Clavijo, 'are a wonder to behold. The soil of the whole province is most fertile, producing great crops of wheat; the livestock are magnificent beasts, and the poultry all of a fine breed.'

Little trace is left of Timur's medieval citadel save for a few uninspiring foundations of the outer walls; the modern city's Theatrical Square has been built over it. Nor does anything remain of Timur's splendid summer palaces. Stripped by robbers and vandals of their faience coverings, the mud-brick walls, domes and arches have simply blown away. Enough does, however, remain of the monumental mosques, madrasas and mausoleums of Timur's legendary 'blue city' to hint at the grandeur that awed Don de Clavijo and other travellers on the Golden Road.

'What Samarkand must have been in its pride,' says Lord Curzon in his book *Russia in Central Asia*, 'when these great fabrics emerged from the mason's hands intact and glittering with all the effulgence of the rainbow, their chambers crowded with students, their sanctuaries thronged with pilgrims, and their corporations endowed by kings, the imagination can still make some endeavour to depict.'

The Madrasas and the Registan

Not much imagination, in fact, is needed to picture the trio of monumental madrasas, which today command three of the four sides of the Registan or central square, as they once were, for since Curzon saw them in ruins in the 1880s, they have been largely restored. And although the Registan does not live up to his much-quoted description of it as 'the noblest public square in the world', it is one of Central Asia's most spectacular sights: surrounded on three sides by the glittering ceramic façades of ancient colleges dominated by giant portals and crowned by dazzling domes, with a tall tiled column in each corner and the fourth side open to the wind.

Monumental buildings arranged around an open square was a typical feature of Timurid town planning, copied later by the Uzbeks and the Safavids of Persia. The madrasa, where the learned men of Islam studied the sciences – some to become prayer leaders and teachers themselves, others to become judges or administrators – was the typical building of the age.

The very concept of the madrasa as an institution separate from the mosque first developed in Central Asia, and so too did some of its distinguishing architectural features. Madrasas were first founded by the eleventh-century Seljuq Turks for the propagation of orthodox Sunni Islam and against heteredox sects and Shiites. The typical plan of the madrasa, with four deep recesses, called *iwans*, arranged around an arcaded courtyard, originated in the region's grand houses. Teachers and students lived and worked in cells and classrooms around the courtyard, similar to Zoroastrian monasteries.

The tradition of the great central gateway fronting the madrasa goes back to the façades of Parthian and Sassanian palaces, where a huge, elaborately decorated entrance symbolizing the power of the kings was intended to overwhelm visitors. The monumental portal of a madrasa was intended, however, to serve a different purpose. For the medieval Muslim builder, a structure was an introvert container, keeping private its interior life, but announcing its presence by an impressive façade. This was articulated by a central portal occupying the whole height of the building and emphasized by flanking columns, while some madrasas also had corner towers at both ends of the façade giving a castle-like look.

The portal has less a spatial but more a volumetric effect, and has no organic connection with the general mass of the building. In fact, entrance is gained through a small door in the façade's great, deeply recessed, central archway, creating a noticeable contrast with the portal itself.

The oldest and – by general agreement – the most beautiful of the three madrasas flanking the Registan is that of Timur's grandson Ulugh Beg, the astronomer. Built by him between 1417 and 1420 on the western side of the square, its portal is twice the height of the present building and spans about two-thirds of its façade. Each end of the portal is finished off with slender, spiral-ribbed pillars, and the façade is flanked by soaring, twin, capitol-topped columns seemingly holding up the azure sky. Ulugh Beg is said to have lectured there in mathematics and astronomy, and the tiles over its large, lancet archway form – appropriately – the shape of stars. Elsewhere, the façade, the inner walls of its recessed archway, and flanking columns, are covered from top to toe in geometric, calligraphic, floral and arabesque patterns picked out in predominantly blue faience mosaic and glazed tiles.

Originally, the Ulugh Beg Madrasa had two storeys, with 50

Behind the imposing façades of Samarkand's madrasas lie enclosed courtyards on to which open what were once the cells of the *ulama*, the wise men of Islam, who wrestled there with the mysteries of science and philosophy.

Goods on sale at Bukhara's open market range from tasty puff pastry cheese triangles and savouries stuffed with mincemeat to reed brushes.

dormitory cells and learning facilities for 100 students. It had four domes crowning the corner cells, and a tall column at each of its four corners. Time, earthquakes and eighteenth-century internecine wars destroyed all four domes, two columns and much of the students' quarters.

Ironically – considering his non-religious beliefs and political affiliation – it was Communist Party leader Lenin who saved the Islamic college of monarchist Ulugh Beg from further deterioration. In 1922 he ordered craftshops set up in Samarkand to produce ceramics to restore its crumbling monuments. And in 1932 he issued instructions for the dangerously leaning northern column of the Ulugh Beg Madrasa to be straightened and reinforced.

More than 200 years elapsed after the building of the Ulugh Beg Madrasa until in the seventeenth century, two more monumental buildings appeared in the Registan: Shirdar and Tilakar madrasas. Both were built on the orders of Amir Yalangtush Bahadur, the then Uzbek ruler of Samarkand, and they took a total of 30 years to complete. More impressive in dimensions than Ulugh Beg Madrasa and more lavishly adorned, they are, nonetheless, somewhat inferior in artistic and architectural terms to their Timurid model.

Facing Ulugh Beg Madrasa, and clearly in imitation of it, the Shirdar or 'lion-bearing', Madrasa was erected between 1619 and 1636. It gets its name from the crude representations of the Persian emblem, the lion – although it resembles more a tiger – leaping across the top of its portal in the rays of the rising sun. Otherwise almost identical in design and decoration, it has the advantage over its opposite of still retaining, on either side of its portal, beautifully proportioned, fluted, twin domes covered with marine-blue tiles. Its flanking columns appear, either by accident or design, to slope outwards giving a false impression of a wider façade.

Closing off the Registan to the north is the Tilakar, or 'gilded' Madrasa, so called because of the amount of gold used in its decoration. Started in 1647 and completed in 1660, when new it must have been the most impressive of the three colleges. Its façade – over 120 m (400 ft) long and 30 m (100 ft) high at its great central portal – has blue dome-topped towers at each end, and is crowned by the dazzling turquoise dome of the grand mosque which forms part of the madrasa. Between the portal and the two end towers extend double

Left The Tilakar, or Gilded, Madrasa takes its name from the richly decorated interior of the mosque attached to it. Painstakingly restored in 1979, the paintwork is already peeling to the left of the mosque's prayer niche because of rising damp caused by the intensive irrigation of Samarkand oasis.

Right A classical arabesque of stylized plant stems, twining upon each other to form an elegant fretted design, decorates the interior of the Tilakar Mosque dome.

rows of lancet archways (narrow and pointed), which give onto what were once dormitory cells.

The most magnificent feature of Tilakar Madrasa is not, however, its impressive exterior, but the interior of its mosque: stunningly decorated in deep blues and gold. Restored in 1979 with almost 1,000 sq m of gilding, the mosque is one of only three buildings in the world where *papier maché* has been used in its interior mouldings. The other two are Bibi Khanum Mosque and Gur-i-Amir mausoleum, both in Samarkand.

The inclusion of a mosque in the Tilakar Madrasa complex is indicative of the increasing emphasis on religious studies in the seventeenth-century Central Asian college curriculum. This reflects the growing power of the *ulama*, influential theologians who advised on politics and law, in relation to the secular rulers, the Amirs, such as would never have been dreamed of in the days when Timur ruled Samarkand.

In Timur's time the Registan, which means 'place in the sand', was a market-place: the official centre of Samarkand where, to the sound of enormous copper pipes called *dzharchis*, heralds proclaimed the beginning and end of wars, and public executions took place. Timur also used the Registan to show off the enormous loot from his victorious campaigns, and to display the spiked heads of defeated enemies.

On sale in the square and adjacent bazaars were not only the rich produce of Samarkand's own vineyards, melon beds and orchards, but also an endless variety of merchandise from far lands as the Castilian envoy, Don de Clavijo, noted:

> From Russia and Tartary come leathers and linens, from Cathay silk stuffs that are the finest in the world. Thence too is brought musk, balas rubies and diamonds, also pearls, lastly rhubarb. From India there are brought spices which are the most costly of the kind, such as nutmegs, cloves, cinnamon and ginger.

Even as recently as the 1920s, a visitor found the Registan like:

> some gorgeous pageant out of the Arabian Nights . . . an absolute kaleidoscope of colouring. The older men wore nothing more sombre than red-striped coats, while the younger ones donned such gay ones – blue, pink, green, yellow, in Bukharian rainbow designs.

Today, however, though groups of Uzbek women in Bukhara rainbow silks still paint an occasional stroke of colour across its cobble-stone expanse, the Registan – even in all its glory – is no longer the heart and soul of Samarkand. In Muslim cities, houses, shops and markets have always crowded up close to the walls of mosques and madrasas, making them a vital part of the community, rather than something separate and apart. In clearing the square and its environments, and landscaping the area around it, the modern planners have overlooked this urban history. As a result, the Registan today is a majestic, skilfully restored museum piece.

Bibi Khanum Mosque

The same is not true of the ruined mosque of Bibi Khanum, which towers like the skeleton of a huge dinosaur over Samarkand's municipal fruit market, whose mounds of melons and piles of pomegranates sprawl right up to its walls. Built in great haste in the last few hectic years of Timur's reign to surpass all other buildings in his vast domains, it was once the largest and most beautiful mosque in Central Asia.

Begun on 11 May, 1399 – a day judged astrologically auspicious – it was built with the loot of Timur's Indian conquests by two hundred architects, artists, master craftsmen and masons assembled from all over the Timurid empire, aided by five hundred labourers and ninety-five elephants from India, which dragged the materials into place. Timur himself is said to have personally supervized final operations from his litter – urging on workmen by throwing them coins and lumps of meat.

Finished after five years of frantic effort, the mosque stood within a capacious courtyard 130 m (432 ft) long and 102 m (338 ft) wide, paved with marble slabs and surrounded by a roofed gallery. Entrance to the high-walled courtyard was gained through great gates made from an amalgam of seven metals, set in a large lancet archway which had a marble base and tiled façade. The gates were flanked by twin, 50-m (168-ft) high ceramic columns.

Facing into the courtyard from left and right were two minor mosques with fluted enamelled domes, and from each of its four corners rose a tall minaret. While at the far end towered the enormous star spangled portal of Bibi Khanum, crowned by a colossal bright blue dome, prompting one chronicler to write: 'Its dome would have been unique had it not been for the heavens, and unique would have been its portal had it not been for the Milky Way.'

Time and history have been merciless to Bibi Khanum. Too hurried construction, according to one witness, caused it to start to crumble even before it was complete, so that the faithful were reluctant to worship there for fear of falling masonry. The mud brick casing of its 2-m (6½-ft) thick cavity walls broke, spilling out rubble infill. An avaricious Uzbek Amir of Bukhara, melted down its metal gates to make coins, and a Russian cannon shell pierced its dome during the battle of Samarkan in 1868. In 1897, an earthquake wreaked further havoc on its dome. It was finally abandoned even by the clergy, and its courtyard was converted into a cotton market.

Today, Bibi Khanum's gauntly beautiful, ruined – but about to be restored – blue dome still dominates Samarkand's skyline. But scaffolding draped around the mosque's great portal partly obscures its ceramic covering of glittering blue and coral coloured stars. The sanctuary's spacious courtyard will, for some time, be cluttered with makeshift workshops and building materials, while a lofty crane bobs – like a giant preying mantis – disconcertingly overhead.

Already the brickwork base of the sanctuary's buildings have been reinforced, the facing of its portals strengthened and its columns straightened. The walls surrounding the courtyard have been rebuilt and the fluted domes of the smaller mosques restored. Original plans had called for the complete rebuilding of the sanctuary, including redecoration of the denuded interior of the great mosque's cavernous dome. However, these plans are now being questioned by some conservationists, who argue that it is better – and cheaper – to restore what remains and leave at least something to the imagination.

Of this mosque there are many legends, chiefly concerning the favourite wife of Timur, Bibi Khanum, from whom it takes its name, and the young Persian architect who designed it. It is said that they fell in love, and he imprinted on her cheek a kiss so passionate that it left a burn. Seeing this, Timur sent his guards to kill the architect, but the Persian fled to the top of the mosque's highest minaret, sprouted wings and flew back to his native Meshed.

As for Bibi Khanum herself, we are again indebted to Don de Clavijo for a vivid description of her appearance at a banquet:

Above Once described as the most beautiful ruin in the world, the grand mosque of Bibi Khanum is now being restored. Built by Timur to surpass in size and grandeur all other structures in his empire, Bibi Khanum still dwarfs modern Samarkand – but not the giant crane repairing its shattered dome.

Below Enduring through time and turmoil, the Gur-i-Amir mausoleum rises from a grove of acacia trees to honour the memory of Timur and his dynastic descendants, including two of his sons and two grandsons.

Far left Restorers' scaffolding sheathing one of the lateral domes of the Bibi Khanum mosque complex partly obscures the elegant calligraphic inscriptions, floral mosaics and glazed brickwork around its base.

Left A giant white marble lectern, made to support a Koran whose pages were more than 2 m (6 ft) tall, stands in the courtyard of the Bibi Khanum mosque complex. It originally stood beneath the mosque's giant dome, but was moved outside because of falling masonry.

She had on a robe of red silk, trimmed with gold lace, long and flowing. It had no waist, and fifteen ladies held up the skirt to enable her to walk. She wore a head-dress of red cloth, very high, covered with large pearls, rubies and emeralds, embroidered with gold lace and surmounted by a tall plume of feathers. Her hair, which was very black, hung down over her shoulders. She was accompanied by 300 ladies-in-waiting, three of whom held her head-dress when she sat down, lest it should tilt over. She had so much white powder on her face that it looked like paper.

Two points in this passage – that she had jet black hair and wore white makeup – would seem to support the general belief that Bibi Khanum was a Chinese princess. The banquet which she and Timur's seven other wives attended was the highlight of a month-long festival – the greatest, according to one account, that Central Asia ever knew – to celebrate the marriage of several of Timur's grandsons, including Ulugh Beg.

Don de Clavijo estimated there were some '20,000 tents pitched in regular streets' in a large meadow on the banks of the Zeravshan to accommodate the guests. Most magnificent were the royal enclosures, surrounded by walls of patterned silk, in each of which stood a large square tent of different colour and design.

Timur's tent was 100 m (332 ft) square, with outer walls of silk woven in bands of white, black and yellow. The ceiling, in the form of a dome, was supported by 12 great tent poles painted blue and gold. It was emblazoned with four eagles with folded wings and topped with a silken turret and simulated battlements which, from a distance, gave it the appearance of a fort.

'Throughout the horde thus encamped,' wrote de Clavijo, 'every craft and art needfull for supply was dispersed', bakers with their ovens, bath houses, and the booths of butchers, cooks, tailors and shoemakers.

When all was prepared, de Clavijo reported, 'Timur loosed the reins of indulgence and pleasure . . . and made red wine flow for all, so that the nobles and people alike swam in its waves'. Abstinence from alcohol appears to be one of the tenets of Islam the Timurids ignored, for 'at none of their feasts', wrote de Clavijo, 'do they consider hilarity attained unless many guests are properly drunk'.

Food at their feasts was mainly meat – mutton and horsemeat

Above Soft light filtering through lattices of carved alabaster falls on Timur's tombstone – a single piece of green jade, dark in contrast to the white marble tombstones of his family surrounding it.

Left The painted ceiling of Hagga Ahrar Mosque, one of the city's few buildings which still serves a religious purpose.

The popular version of the legend of the architect of the Bibi Khanum Mosque in Samarkand has it that he was found flirting with Timur's favourite wife, and escaped the ruler's wrath by sprouting wings and flying from one of the mosque's minarets. However, the official version, shown here in a Persian-style miniature painting from Timur's authorized biography, is that he was caught and hung. By permission of the British Library.

roasted, boiled and stewed, knots of horse tripe and balls of forced meat as big as a fist, and whole sheep's heads – piled on huge leather platters so heavy they had to be dragged along the ground.

Entertainment consisted of acrobats and dancers, wrestlers and jesters, singers and musicians, and performing horses and elephants.

But while wishing to give pleasure to the people, de Clavijo reported, Timur also wanted to make an example of those who had displeased him. So a gallows was set up in the great tent city on which, among others, was hanged the Mayor of Samarkand, who Timur charged had betrayed his trust whilst he was away fighting the Ottoman Turks, and oppressed the people.

Also hanged were two officials Timur had left in charge of the construction of the Bibi Khanum Mosque. Details of their crimes are not documented, although Timur is reported to have been unhappy with the sanctuary gateway, which he ordered torn down and rebuilt.

Timur was also dissatisfied with the mausoleum he was building for his favourite grandson, Muhammad Sultan, who died fighting the Ottomans. This too he ordered demolished and rebuilt – within ten days; a miracle that the builders, in fear of their lives, reportedly accomplished.

No sooner had this been finished than Timur embarked on yet another breakneck building project: the construction of a bazaar in which all kinds of merchandise – usually sold separately – could be displayed in a single street: a kind of medieval supermarket.

Heedless of the protests of their occupants, all houses on the site indicated by Timur were torn down. Masons working in relays round the clock laid a new street, put up shops on either side, and covered it with a domed roof with windows to let in the light. 'The tumult day and night was such', wrote Don de Clavijo, 'that it seemed all the devils of hell were at work there'. But within 20 days the bazaar was not only complete, but the merchants were already open for business.

Timur's Mausoleum

Finally satisfied with his city, Timur set off in January 1405 with 200,000 men on his greatest venture: to break through the Great Wall and conquer China – then the richest country in the world. But 640 km (400 miles) march from Samarkand he suddenly fell ill and died, on a cold winter's day in February, aged 69. His body, perfumed with rose

Right Part of the giant sextant which was set in a hillside overlooking Samarkand, and with which Timur's grandson, the celebrated astronomer Ulugh Beg, plotted the positions of over 1000 stars without the aid of a telescope. Degrees are still clearly recorded on the marble cladding of the massive stone instrument.

Far right Visible from afar, the Koranic inscription, 'There is no God but Allah, and Muhammad is his prophet', is traced in huge white kufic, the most majestic of early calligraphic scripts, around the base of the elegant ribbed dome of Guri-i-Amir.

Left and above right All the blues of heaven and earth – from the darkest mauves to the palest opalescent – are said to be gathered in this narrow passageway flanked by royal tombs of the Timurid dynasty at Shah-i-Zinda.

Below Six centuries of sun, wind and rain have failed to dim the lustre of these tiles adorning one of the royal tombs at Shah-i-Zinda.

Above The entrance to Hazrati Shah-i-Zinda – the Shrine of the Living King – from which the Timurid royal cemetery of Samarkand takes its name. The saint buried here, Qasim ibn Abbas, converted Sogdiana to Islam at the time of the seventh-century Arab conquests.

Below Shah-i-Zinda has been a place of pilgrimage since the eleventh century. Following tradition, these two Uzbek women, their heads draped reverently in white shawls, touch a sacred stone at the entrance to the saint's shrine.

water, musk and camphor, was placed in a coffin decorated with pearls and precious stones and dispatched in the dead of night – so not to unsettle his troops – to his beloved Samarkand.

Timur was buried in the mausoleum he had built – and rebuilt – for his grandson Muhammad Sultan, which from then on became the Timurid dynasty sepulchre known as Gur-i-Amir – the Ruler's Tomb. But Timur did not, reportedly, rest easy there until the captive craftsmen who had built it were freed. According to Johann Schiltberger, a Bavarian squire who served Timur for many years:

> After he was buried the priests that served the temple heard Timur howl every night for a year. Finally, they went to his son and begged that he set free the prisoners taken by his father in other countries, especially those craftsmen he had brought to his capital to work. He let them go, and as soon as they were free Timur did not howl any more.

Like the madrasa, the Muslim monumental tomb is an architectural creation of Central Asia that has been imitated all round the Islamic realm. Composed of cylinders, domes or cones, and polyhedrons, these medieval mausoleums are worthy examples of pure geometrical art. And Gur-i-Amir is among the finest.

Built of mud brick and faced with coloured glaze, faience mosaic and ceramic tiles of different colours and design, Gur-i-Amir is composed of an octagonal hall, crowned by a fluted cantaloup-shaped dome atop a cylindrical base. The dome is overlaid with turquoise tiles decorated with dark blue and yellow motifs, while around its base the inscription 'There is no God but Allah, and Muhammed is his prophet' is traced in large white calligraphic characters outlined in dark blue.

The mausoleum stands behind an impressive portal flanked by twin, ceramic-covered columns, in a small sanctuary set in a quiet tree-shaded square. It is surrounded by humble houses and alleys that have yet to be bulldozed down. Inside the sepulchre, a darkened passage leads to the domed octagonal hall, which is 35 m (115 ft) in height. Soft light filters through fretted openings, illuminating the gilded dome and falling on tiled and carved niches, and plaster inscriptions describing Timur's genealogy and heroic deeds.

Up to eye level the walls of the chamber are clad with green alabaster hexagon tiles, while higher up, the hall is ringed with alternating bands of eulogistic calligraphy and blue and gold geometric paintwork. The dome, almost Moorish in decor, is gilded with 3 km (6½ lb) of gold.

Beneath the dome is a stone railing enclosing seven tombstones, the centre one of which – darker in contrast to the others, which are of white marble – is that of Timur. 'Only a stone, and my name upon it', Timur is said to have whispered as he laying dying. It is, however, no ordinary stone, but a massive monolith of dark green, almost black, jade intricately carved. It is said to have been sent to Samarkand from the mountains of Chinese Turkestan by a Mongolian princess. This tombstone, which measures 1.8 m (6 ft) in length, 43 cm (17 in) wide and 35 cm (14 in) thick, is the largest known specimen of jade in existence.

Beneath the hall is a crypt where the actual graves are located. And there lies yet another legend. Popular belief has long held that whoever disturbed Timur's grave would bring down upon his country an invader more terrible than Timur himself. Ignoring this, however, the distinguished Soviet scientist, Mikhail Gerasimov, exhumed the body. His examination of the skeleton confirmed that Timur, as his name implies, was lame in one leg. But, the story goes, as the professor was examining Timur's skull, on 22 June, 1941, one of his assistants burst into the crypt and announced that Hitler's armies had invaded Russia.

Next to Timur is buried his spiritual mentor, Mir (sage) Sayid Bereke, which is why the mausoleum is sometimes referred to as Gur-i-Mir. Also buried there are Timur's youngest son and successor, Shah Rukh, and his grandson Ulugh Beg. Emerging victorious from a five-year family power struggle in the wake of Timur's death, Shah Rukh chose Herat, in present-day Afghanistan as his official residence, and appointed his son Ulugh Beg as viceroy of Samarkand.

Ulugh Beg's Observatory

During his rule – from 1409 to his assassination 40 years later, Ulugh Beg made his grandfather's capital into an intellectual gathering place for astronomers, poets, theologians and architects. Behind the tiled façades of Samarkand's madrasas, mathematicians and religious philosophers wrestled with the mysteries of meaning, while the circular observatory that Ulugh Beg built on a hill overlooking the city housed the finest astronomers of the age.

Babur, the last Timurid ruler of Samarkand, described Ulugh Beg's observatory as a three-storey, tile-faced structure at least 30 m (99 ft) high and 46 m (152 ft) in diametre. Set in a trench, 2 m (6½ ft) wide and 11 m (36 ft) deep cut into the hillside, and aligned with one of the earth's meridians, was a giant sextant with a radius of 40 m (132 ft) and an arc 63 m (208 ft) long. With this instrument and the naked eye – telescopes were not yet invented – Ulugh Beg and his fellow astronomers plotted the course coordinates of 1,018 stars observed in the clear night sky over the Kara Kum desert. They also measured the coordinates of the sun, the moon and the planets, and determined – with amazing accuracy – the length of the year.

Ulugh Beg's star chart was the first precise map of the heavens to be produced. His calculations, translated into Latin, were widely studied in Europe, and also used by Chinese astrologers. His remarkably accurate calender – within a minute of the modern calculation of 365 days, 6 hours, 9 minutes and 9.6 seconds – brought him posthumous honour in the West when it was published in 1652 at Oxford.

Ulugh Beg's observatory was destroyed by fanatics after his murder, and for centuries its whereabouts remained a mystery, until in 1908, after many years of painstaking study of ancient manuscripts, the Soviet historian Vladamir Vyatkin succeeded in unearthing the lower part of the sextant. On the marble cladding of this massive stone instrument the degrees are still recorded in almost as perfect condition as the day they were cut. And fragments of the metal rails upon which the instrument moved are still in place.

A small, circular museum documenting Ulugh Beg's achievements has been built on the hilltop over the ruins of his observatory, and such is the medieval monarch's standing in modern Samarkand that it is customary for newly-wed couples to visit there immediately after their nuptials.

Shah-i-Zinda

Another place of pilgrimage on another low hill overlooking Samarkand is Hazrati Shah-i-Zinda, Shrine of the Living King, a cluster of elegant mortuary chapels where the finest glaze decor in all of Central Asia is found.

A place of pilgrimage since the eleventh century, Timur rebuilt it as a royal cemetery for his family and friends, clothing their mausoleums, both inside and out, with vivid mosaic panels, exquisitely embossed tiles, carved ceramic columns and brilliantly polished brickwork. The royal cemetery is reached through a large gateway at the foot of the hill, where 36 large stone steps, worn smooth by the feet of pilgrims, climb steeply to the tombs. Midway up the flight, on a terrace to the left, stands a blue-domed mausoleum variously attributed to Ulugh Beg's tutor and Timur's nurse.

At the head of the steps a white arch leads through to a paved passage, and this is flanked on both sides by tombs and mortuary chapels luminescent in blue tiles. It is said that on this narrow alley are all the blues known to heaven and earth – from the darkest of the ocean depths to the palest of the farthest sky. And as you walk among them, this sea of blues wash about you in rich patterns of calligraphic and geometric design.

Besides their refined beauty, the mausoleums of Shah-i-Zinda represent a unique record of the development of Timurid ceramic art and architecture, and the changes it underwent due to the influence of captured artists and architects from foreign lands. The mausoleum of Timur's sister Shirin-beka-aka, built in 1385, represents, for example, a new trend in design and decoration at the end of the fourteenth century due to the influence of architects Timur brought from Khwarzm. To give greater character to the building there are two cupolas, the second on a drum base whose sixteen sides are visible from both inside and outside the edifice. Also there is the novel use of carved, glazed mosaic for decoration. In the mausoleum of one of Timur's wives, Tuman-aka, built at the beginning of the fifteenth century, a beamed vault replaced the traditional tier of arches, and the proportions of the interior are enhanced by tall, rather wide and shallow niches.

Tuman-aka's tomb stands, with four others, in a small courtyard at the end of the mausoleum-flanked passageway, and is reached through an archway, in the right side of which is set a carved wooden door which leads to the early fourteenth century shrine of Qasim ibn Abbas – the Living King. His tomb is approached through several ante-chambers decorated with plasterwork and supported by carved wooden pillars, and including a small prayer hall lined with diamond and star shaped blue and green tiles. The tomb itself takes the form of a stone swathed in a shawl only visible through a grating, and it still forms a place of pilgrimage.

Many different legends revolve around Qasim ibn Abbas, a

descendant of the Prophet Muhammad who converted Sogdiana to Islam at the time of the seventh-century Arab conquests. But most concur that he jumped with his severed head – either chopped off by Zorastorian fire worshippers or removed by himself – into a nearby well where he lives to this day ready to emerge again to defend Islam. His failure to appear when the Communists siezed Samarkand has, however, somewhat shaken his reputation.

3 Divine Bukhara

Although it is for rugs that Bukhara is now best known, it was as 'Divine Bukhara' – with its hundreds of mosques, madrasas and minarets – that Flecker and the Muslim world remembered it.

The 40-year rule of Timur's son Shah Rukh, a devout Muslim and a man of peace, saw the transformation of his father's restless nomad empire into an orthodox Sunni Muslim state with Herat as its capital, Samarkand as its intellectual centre, and Bukhara as its holiest city.

When Shah Rukh died in 1477, his son Ulugh Beg, who had governed both Bukhara and Samarkand during his father's reign, briefly ascended the Timurid throne. Two years later, however, Ulugh Beg was murdered by his own son, Abd al-Latif, who shortly afterwards was himself murdered by his cousin Abdullah, who in turn was overthrown by another cousin, Abu Sayid.

Weakened by these internal power struggles, the empire Timur had fought so hard to create disintegrated, and the fertile Zeravshan valley fell easy prey to yet another wave of nomads – the Uzbeks – bursting from the steppe. By 1500, under their leader Muhammad Shaibani, a descendant of Genghiz Khan's grandson Shaiban, they had captured Samarkand and Bukhara, and made the land between the Amu Darya and Syr Darya rivers their national homeland – which it remains today.

The Uzbeks, who had converted to Islam early in the fourteenth century, continued to build handsome mosques and madrasas in Bukhara and Samarkand. Large and elaborate, they lacked the purity and harmony of style and decoration of their Timurid predecessors.

However, under the Janid dynasty, which succeeded the Shaibanids in 1599 and ruled Uzbekistan from Bukhara for the next two hundred years, Bukhara became a great centre of religion and learning, with some 360 mosques and 80 madrasas supported by rich endowments.

Pilgrims and students flocked to Bukhara from India and Kashmir, from Persia and the Arab lands, and from Russia and the cities of eastern Turkestan. By the end of the eighteenth century Bukhara is said to have had 30,000 students and the atmosphere of a great university city that had few equals in the world at that time. In the 1800s, however, the Russians began to advance into Central Asia, and by 1900 had conquered it all. Bukhara was absorbed into the czarist empire in 1868, and became isolated from the Muslim world. Finally, in 1920, the communists overthrew its feudal rulers and closed down all but one of its madrasas and a handful of its mosques.

Towers, not minarets, and therefore never used to call the faithful to prayer, these four bulbous structures surmount the gateway of a former madrasa misnamed Char Minar – Four Minarets.

Although under Mikhail Gorbachev some mosques have reopened for worship, Bukhara is no longer a centre of pilgrimage or religious learning. Nor it is, as Lord Curzon found it in the 1880s, 'the most interesting city in the world'. Socialism, however, has not yet totally extinguished the old way of life. Part of the city is still as Curzon described it: 'a wilderness of crooked alleys, winding irregularly between the blind walls of clay-built houses'. And it is still possible to see elderly Bukhariots 'walk abroad with the dignity of a patriarch and in the garb of a prince' – colourful striped coat, knee-high leather boots, and patterned turban.

Furthermore, Bukhara's ancient monuments – built over a millennium – are unlike the relatively recent buildings of Khiva, which have been restored to within an inch of their life; or the fourteenth to fifteenth century monuments of Samarkand, which are crudely incorporated in a modern city. Instead, they form a pleasing and harmonious whole.

The 'Ark'

The ancient cities of Turkestan had three components: the *shahristan*, or city proper, inhabited by aristocrats and artisans; the citadel, within the *shahristan*, where the ruler lived with his entourage; and the *rabad*, adjacent to the *shahristan*, where commercial activity took place. The layout of Bukhara, however, is slightly different as its citadel is outside the *shahristan*, but contiguous with it. Surrounded by high crenellated walls 6 m (20 ft) thick, this 1,000-year-old mud-brick fortress, known as the 'Ark', contains palaces, mosques, harems and offices, and is entered by a steep, dark, winding passageway flanked by sinister torture cells.

Although much of it was destroyed when the last amir, Sayid Alim, set fire to it before fleeing to escape the Communists, the Ark's imposing entrance gate, flanked by twin turrets, has been restored. Over this gate once hung a great clock made in the last century by the Italian watchmaker, Giovanni Orlando, to satisfy the mechanical passion of Amir Nasrullah. But once the clock was set up, Nasrullah had Orlando beheaded because, some say, he refused to embrace Islam, or, according to others, the clock stopped.

Two Britons who fell foul of Nasrullah were Colonel Charles Stoddart and Captain Arthur Conolly, players in the Great Game – the nineteenth-century espionage war between Britain and Russia for

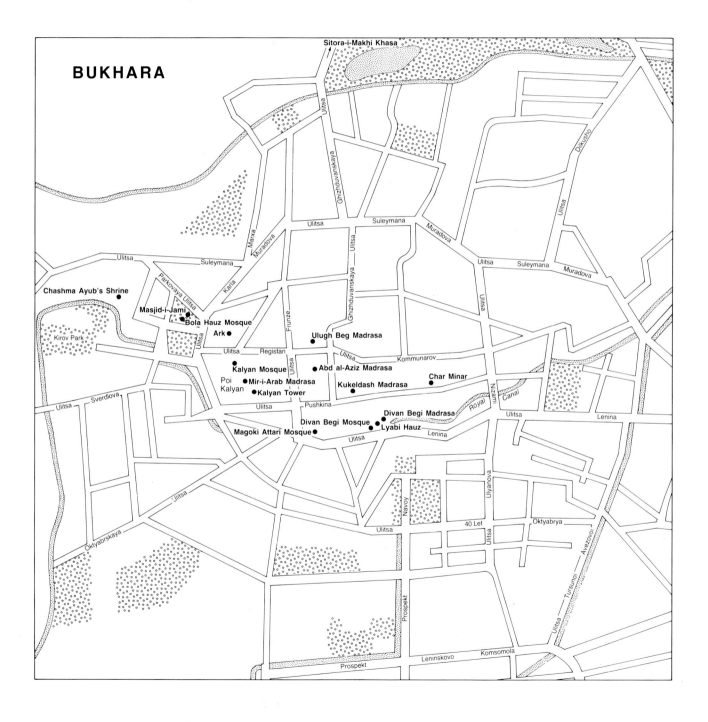

BUKHARA

Sitora-i-Makhi Khasa

Chashma Ayub's Shrine

Masjid-i-Jami

Bola Hauz Mosque
Ark

Kirov Park

Ulugh Beg Madrasa

Kalyan Mosque

Abd al-Aziz Madrasa

Poi
Kalyan   Mir-i-Arab Madrasa   Kukeldash Madrasa   Char Minar

Kalyan Tower

Divan Begi Madrasa

Divan Begi Mosque

Magoki Attari Mosque   Lyabi Hauz

Ulitsa Marxa
Ulitsa Muradova
Ulitsa Suleymana
Ulitsa Ghizhduvanskaya
Ulitsa Muradova
Dikusho
Ulitsa
Ulitsa Suleymana   Muradova
Parkovaya Ulitsa
Ulitsa Suleymana
Ulitsa Karla
Frunze
Ulitsa Ghizhduvanskaya
Ulitsa
Registan
Ulitsa
Kommunarov
Ulitsa
Sverdlova
Pushkina
Royal Canal
Nizami
Ulitsa
Lenina
Lenina
Oktyabrskaya
Ulitsa
Ulyanova
Navoy
40 Let   Oktyabrya
Ulitsa
Tursunoi
Avezovoi
Ulitsa
Prospekt
Prospekt   Leninskovo   Komsomola

Above Bukhara's most famous landmark, the twelfth-century Kalyan Tower, dwarfs even the giant blue-tiled dome and monumental portal of the seventeenth-century Mir-i-Arab Madrasa. Together with the massive Kalyan Mosque, these buildings make up the city's main religious complex, Poi Kalyan, or Pedestal of the Great One; the 'Great One' being the Kalyan Tower, and the 'Pedestal' the small square in which it and the other two buildings stand.

Below Although Bukhara is no longer a centre of pilgrimage and learning – it owes its present prosperity to deposits of natural gas and tourism – the Kalyan Tower and the twin domes of the Mir-i-Arab religious college still dominate the city's skyline. In the background is the verdant oasis that has supported Bukhara for over two millenium.

control of Central Asia, fictionalized in Rudyard Kipling's *Kim*. Stoddart was sent to Bukhara in 1842 to try and forge an alliance with the amir against the Russians, but he offended Nasrullah by approaching his palace on horseback instead of deferentially on foot. The amir found Conolly, who attempted to effect Stoddart's pardon, equally offensive and so beheaded them both.

The remains of the two British officers, along with those of the other victims of the bloodthirsty amir, today lie buried in long-forgotten graves beneath the dusty Registan, where Uzbek boys play football, in the shadow of the now symbolic citadel.

The czar's envoy, Prince Ferdinand ze Sayn-Wittgenstein-Berlebourg, received a more courteous reception when he visited Amir Mazaffer el-Din in 1882. Although, as Henri Moser, a Swiss who accompanied him to Bukhara, reported, the amir still demanded deference and dealt summarily with offenders:

> The amir received the guests clad in an ill-designed uniform with all types of gold orders embellishing it. He had, however, a magnificent green cashmere turban. Once the reception was over the *dastarkhan*, or official feast, was served in a very drafty pavilion, and gifts of fur-lined gold brocade and silk cloaks were sent to the visitors to keep them warm. Etiquette, however, required them to leave the cloaks flung over a chair indicating that the light of the amir's presence was sufficient to banish all thought of cold.

Later, Moser watched from his bedroom window, 'by way of distraction', as those who had incurred the amir's wrath were hurled to their death from Bukhara's highest building: the twelfth-century Kalyan Tower. Also known as the Tower of Death, this slender, soaring structure, despite its notoreity, is designated by the United Nations Educational, Scientific and Cultural Organization (UNESCO) as a historical monument worthy of preservation as part of the world's cultural heritage.

Bukhara's Decorative Brickwork

This tapering tower, topped by an enclosed viewing rotunda, is built of honey-coloured bricks laid in alternate protruding and receding planes and at varying angles to create intricate geometrical patterns that appear to change with the slant of the sun's rays. Ten broad and six narrow bands of different patterned brickwork, occasionally inlaid with blue or bottle green tiles, ring the tower producing a texture like that of an elaborately knitted sweater.

Built in 1127, the tower rises to a height of nearly 45 m (150 ft) over Bukhara's main religious complex, Poi Kalyan, and besides being a place of execution it also served as a minaret, from where the faithful were called to prayer; and in times of war – which were frequent – it was used as a watchtower, to warn of the approaching enemy.

An even earlier example of decorative brickwork is the tenth-century tomb of the Persian Samanid dynasty, who made Bukhara their capital. Small, and strikingly simple, it consists of a cube-shaped building with corner columns supporting a squat dome, and is one of the finest examples of early medieval architecture. Its architectural principles, including a dome set on a cuneiform (wedge-shaped) drum, were followed in Central Asia for five centuries.

Buried for hundreds of years, the tomb of the Samanids was rediscovered in 1930 during landscaping of the Kirov Park of Rest and Culture, and was restored using bricks made of clay bound with egg yoke and camel's milk, to match the originals.

Most of Bukhara's ancient monuments – like those of Samarkand – are made of mud brick, which was the only building material readily available to medieval architects in desert regions. Wood from the oases could be used only sparingly – mainly for pillars and lintels – and stone had to be transported from mountain quarries hundreds of kilometres away.

Today, although modern building materials are easily obtainable in Bukhara, mud bricks are still made, within a few hundred metres of the Samanid dynasty mausoleum, much as they were 1000 years ago. The main ingredients are still dirt from the surrounding desert, and water from the river Zeravshan, although the modern binding agent beniton has replaced egg yoke and camel's milk. And, as in the past, the bricks are still made by hand – very much like children making mud pies – in simple wooden moulds, but instead of being left for months to dry in the sun, they are now baked for a day in a kiln at a temperature of 700° centigrade.

The mud bricks are made by a small cooperative for the restoration of Bukhara's ancient buildings. And each consignment is made to

Modernization has not totally extinguished the old way of life in Bukhara, where it is still possible to witness scenes similar to those described by Lord Curzon over 100 years ago, including men who 'walk abroad with the dignity of a patriarch and in the garb of a prince'.

special order because, says manager Salemov Hayroglu, although to the inexperienced eye all the bricks look similar, 'each monument has its special needs. Each period had its own size and type of bricks for both inside and outside the buildings'.

A closer inspection of the tomb of the Samanids, with its bricks laid here as rosettes and there as squares and triangles, quickly confirms this.

A Centre of Learning and Commerce

Under the Samanids, whose empire stretched from Herat in the east to Isfahan in the west, Bukhara became an important commercial and cultural centre. Hoards of Samanid coins have been found as far afield as Scandinavia; the court languages were Persian, Arabic and Turkish; and, at a time when manuscripts were 'published' only through the tedious labour of copyists, it had several private libraries that were open to the public. One of these was the royal library about which Ibn Sina (Avincenna), writing 1000 years ago, said:

> I found there many rooms filled with books which were arranged in cases, row upon row. One room was allotted to works of Arabic philology and poetry, another to jurisprudence and so forth, the books of each particular science having a room to themselves. I inspected the catalogue of ancient Greek authors; I saw in this collection books of which few people have heard even the names, and which I myself have never seen either before or since.

All trace of this and Bukhara's other eleventh-century libraries have now disappeared, but Ibn Sina's works, based on his studies there, are still read in medical and pharmacological circles.

On the edge of Kirov Park, and overlooking Bukhara's colourful open market, stands the shrine of Chashma Ayub, or Job's Spring, built on the site of a miraculous spring which is said to have gushed forth at the behest of the prophet Job. Its foundations date from the twelfth century, although considerable alterations have been made since, and its most striking feature is a conical dome quite atypical of Bukhara.

Vendors' stalls displaying gaudy felt rugs and Bukhara rainbow silks reach to within a few metres of Chashma Ayub, contrasting sharply with its stark construction: a plain oblong building, with three small domes, and a conical cupola on a tall cylindrical base.

Overleaf left One of the finest achievements of early medieval architecture, the mausoleum of the tenth-century Samanid rulers of Bukhara features intricate brickwork decor and a dome set on a cuneiform drum: decorative and architectural styles that were followed in Central Asia for five centuries.

Overleaf above right The view over Bukhara from the modern water tower by Bola Hauz: the twin-turreted entrance and crenellated walls of its ancient citadel, with the domes and tower of Poi Kalyan in the background, and beyond them the city's modern districts.

Overleaf below right A conical cupola quite atypical of Bukhara tops the shrine of Chashma Ayub. The foundation of the building dates back to the twelfth century, but considerable alterations have been made since, including a new entrance and oblong exterior walls added in the sixteenth century, giving it a somewhat stark, ascetic look.

From Chashma Ayub the stalls of the open market, which sell everything from fresh fruit to embroidered Uzbek skull caps, sprawl across a dusty expanse to the crumbling remains of the once proud walls – 12 km (7½ miles) long and 10 m (33 ft) high – that until 50 years ago ringed the city.

Bukhara's earthen walls, like the rest of the city, were considered 'divine'. 'Whoever says Bukhara's walls are not straight', goes an old Central Asian saying, 'he is cast out by God'. And even as recently as 1938 a British visitor found them and their 'battlements, eleven gates and watchtowers still standing in all their crumbling magnificence'.

Since then, however, the gates have been pulled down to make way for modern roads into the city. The battlements and watchtowers have collapsed, and much of the walls have been demolished to improve, the planners say, air circulation.

Eleven caravan trails once passed through Bukhara's eleven gates bringing a vast range of goods from all points of the compass to be sold in the city's bustling bazaars. These covered bazaars, located near the gates which served the trade routes, or near places of worship where people always gathered, were among the richest in Central Asia. The disintegration of Timur's empire, however, led to a failure of law and order along the trade routes. Fierce Turkmen raiders ranged freely over the Kara Kum desert ambushing the richly laden caravans, with the result that transcontinental trade, which has long been Central Asia's principle source of prosperity, declined. Furthermore, the Portuguese discovery, in the late fifteenth century, of the sea route around the Cape of Good Hope quickly led to direct trade between Europe and the Far East, and the one-time middleman, Central Asia, was no longer the crossroads of the world.

Now, like its walls, little is left of Bukhara's teeming bazaars, except clusters of small cascading domes beneath which shops that once dealt in precious stones, silks and furs now do a meagre trade in mundane modern items and tourist souvenirs.

Bukhara's covered bazaars and narrow streets were influenced by its hot, arid climate. It has always been a city seeking shade – and water. This is carried from the Zeravshan river, which skirts round the city, via the Royal Canal, and is transported through the city by a network of open channels linked to large pools, or 'tanks', which form natural gathering-places.

Lyabi Hauz – the Nucleus of the Old City

Bukhara's largest 'tank', Lyabi Hauz or Holy Pool, forms the nucleus of the old city, and is surrounded by ancient mulberry trees whose spreading branches provide shade for the grateful citizens who flock there to meet their friends. On the shaded terraces around the square pool are open-air tea-houses and eating-places, where beared old men in striped coats and colourful turbans sit cross-legged on raised wooden platforms – looking very much like bedsteads – sipping strong black tea and eating bowls of steaming *pilav*, the traditional rice and lamb dish of Central Asia.

Holy Pool is flanked on three sides by mosques and madrasas, one of which, the sixteenth-century Kukeldash Madrasa, is – at 80 by 60 m (265 by 199 ft) – the largest, and one of the plainest, in Central Asia. Facing each other across the other two sides are, by contrast, the colourful portals of the Divan Begi Mosque and madrasa, the latter featuring large birds of prey in faience mosaic above its central arch.

Like the mosques and madrasas of Samarkand, those of Bukhara have, in the centre of their façade, a portal reaching the whole height of the building, forming the entrance to a cell-lined courtyard in the case of the madrasa, and a domed prayer hall in the case of the mosque.

But while in Samarkand many former religious buildings are preserved as museums, in Bukhara they are mainly put to secular use. The Kukeldash Madrasa, for example, served for many years as a depository for the municipal archives, while the Divan Begi Mosque is now a gallery for local art and crafts, and the courtyard of the Divan Begi Madrasa features a quiet cafe.

Along the fourth side of Lyabi Hauz runs the Royal Canal, and parallel to it there is a paved pedestrian mall with shops along one side. The mall, said to be a section of the Golden Road, leads through a domed archway, where merchants once changed money before entering the bazaars, to Magoki-Attari, Bukhara's oldest mosque. A small, domed building, Magoki-Attari is noted for the complex geometric patterns executed in carved ceramic on its twelfth-century portal, and its simple six-columned interior.

The renovation of the general-purpose area around Lyabi Huaz, which combines the restoration of ancient monuments with the creation of modern facilities but without loss of charm, is one of the best examples of preservation in the region.

Some of the patterns created by early medieval builders simply by laying mud-bricks at varying angles and in alternate protruding and receding planes. From the tomb of the tenth-century Samanid rulers of Bukhara.

Left The slender, tapering Kalyan Tower soars to a height of about 45 m (150 ft). Built of honey-coloured bricks arranged in different patterned bands, the tower is on UNESCO's list of historical monuments that should be preserved as part of the world's cultural heritage.

Above From the arched openings around the Kalyan Tower's graceful rotunda, *muzeines* once called the faithful to prayer five times a day, sentries kept watch for the enemy when Bukhara was at war, and condemned prisoners were hurled to their deaths on the flagstones below – a practise which earned it the name 'Tower of Death'.

Poi Kalyan

The best thing about the area around Bukhara's other major ancient architectural complex, Poi Kalyan, is that it has been left virtually alone.

Apart from the unlikely new name of 'Kommunarov', the street leading to Poi Kalyan is still a narrow, bustling thoroughfare with a raised, veranda-covered sidewalk to protect pedestrians from the summer sun and winter slush, where old men in turbans sit gossiping in front of a row of pale blue painted shops. A stork's nest is sited crazily atop one of the complex's three blue domes, and the square between its monuments serves as a playground for the local junior school.

Poi Kalyan means 'Pedestal of the Great One', the 'Great One' being the Kalyan Tower, and the 'Pedestal' the small square over which it looms, dwarfing even the monumental mosque and madrasa which face each other across it.

The Mir-i-Arab Madrasa, built in 1535 by Shaikh Mir-i-Arab, is the only functioning religious college left in Bukhara, and through the fretted screen at its entrance – which is closed to the public – one can still glimpse the seminarists pursuing their studies in the cloistered courtyard, surrounded by the cells in which they live. Its façade, featuring the usual large central arch, flanked on either side by a double row of smaller ones, has lost most of its ceramic facing, but the twin blue-tiled domes either side of its portal have been restored.

So too has the portal of the Kalyan Mosque opposite, which features panels of elegant white Arabic script on a dark blue background, set in a sea of small yellow flowers and turquoise stars made from thousands of tiny pieces of faience mosaic. Rich floral patterns also decorate the central arch and area above it.

This magnificent portal leads, by way of a gate in its central arch, to a spacious courtyard surrounded on three sides by a roofed and deeply recessed gallery, which provided shelter from the elements for worshippers. On the fourth side, facing the entrance, stands another imposing portal of polished blue and beige brick, with engaged pillars (attached, or sunk into the wall) at each end in dark blue, green and gold, which leads to a richly decorated ceramic *mirhab*, or prayer niche, beneath a high blue dome.

Built in the fifteenth century by the Shaibanid khans and modelled on the Bibi Khanum Mosque at Samarkand, the Kalyan was once

Above Lyabi Hauz, or Holy Pool, is the nucleus of the old city. Surrounded by ancient mulberry trees, giving much-needed shade, it is a natural gathering place. And the buildings overlooking it, such as the Divan Begi Mosque, now used as a gallery to display local crafts, serve as a focus for Bukhara's cultural life.

Below 'Whoever says Bukhara's walls are not straight', goes the old Central Asian saying, 'he is cast out by God'. Now only these crumbling earthworks remain of the 12 km (7.4 miles) of 10 m (33 ft) high battlements that once ringed the city.

Above On shaded terraces around Lyabi Hauz, bearded old Bukhariots in striped coats and colourful turbans sit on raised platforms sipping strong black tea with their friends.

Below This carved marble spout once supplied water, brought from the Zeravshan river by a network of open channels, to one of Bukhara's now-abandoned neighbourhood pools.

Bukhara's biggest mosque, with room in its courtyard for 10,000 worshippers. Today it is an empty haven for playful swifts, which wheel in and out of its arches and around its towering dome.

Behind Poi Kalyan, a cluster of small cascading domes covers a small bazaar, beyond which, facing each other across a narrow lane, stand the madrasas of Ulugh Beg and the Janid ruler Abd al-Aziz. Bukhara's earliest madrasa, the Ulugh Beg, was already functioning as a religious college in 1417. Abd al-Aziz Madrasa was built more than two centuries later. Of the two, though the later building is larger and more elaborate, the earlier one has greater purity and harmony of style and decoration. Both, however, retain some of their former splendour, their façades still decorated with the original, intricate arabesque tiles.

Islamic Ceramic Art

Although fine ceramic art no longer flourishes in Bukhara, the small cooperative near the tomb of the Samanids does still produce glazed brick and slab for the restoration of the city's ancient monuments. Coloured glazes are mixed from seven ingredients, including pigments. The glaze is painted in a thin layer onto baked mud brick and fired for one day or more – depending on the colour – at 1000°C, in a process which has remained virtually unchanged throughout the ages.

The Mesopotamians were the first people to use glaze as a construction material. They used it to make mud walls water resistant rather than as decoration. But glaze allowed the introduction of colour, and these colourful surfaces, decorated with beautiful geometric and floral forms, arabesque panels and elegant bands of calligraphy, eventually became an indispensable element of Islamic architecture, absorbing the creative genius that, in the Christian West, went into frescoes and sculpture.

In architecture there are two kinds of glazed material: slab and brick. Slabs can be used as tiles, to cover large continuous surfaces, or as mosaics to cover every kind of surface, flat or curved. The preparation of glazed brick is simple: the baked brick is dipped into, or painted with, coloured glaze and put into a kiln. For faience mosaic, larger slabs are prepared from which small pieces are cut and glazed.

Faience mosaic originated in the simple patterned brick decoration of Central Asia, which itself evolved into the intricate coating of surfaces with small, variously shaped, different-coloured pieces of terracotta.

Left Behind the protective portal of Divan Begi Madrasa theological students from all over Central Asia, Iran, India and Chinese Turkestan once worked in quiet seclusion. Today, however, like most of Bukhara's other former religious buildings, Divan Begi serves a secular purpose as a busy courtyard cafe.

Below Two birds of prey, picked out in thousands of tiny pieces of faience mosaic, soar over the great archway entrance of Divan Begi Madrasa, overlooking the shaded terraces of Lyabi Hauz.

Characteristic of the design of seventeenth-century Central Asia madrasas, a double row of small arches flanks both sides of the large central arch in Divan Begi's façade.

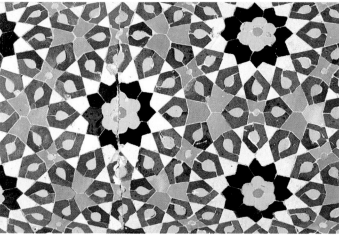

Above Once a great university city with many theological colleges and over 30,000 students from all over the Muslim east, Bukhara now has only one functioning religious school, Mir-i-Arab Madrasa, with only 80 students. However, because of the new religious freedom under Mikhail Gorbachev, this is being increased to 200.

Below The most common of the four main styles of ceramic decor used in Bukhara is floral. These two patterns are among the many floral mosaics that decorate the Kalyan Mosque.

This technique is quite distinctive from the art of glazed tiles, although frequently – even from a short distance – the visual effect is similar.

Tiles are prepared to fit certain wall surfaces. The design on the tiles is prepared in place, and sent to a workshop. The coarse tile bodies are usually covered by a fine layer of earth called 'slip' into which paintings are made.

There are three techniques for applying design and glaze onto tiles: coloured glaze, underglaze and overglaze painting. In the first, the patterns are drawn on the tile surface by a special material which, in the kiln, gains in relief and prevents the different colours from running. Here the colour itself becomes glaze. In the underglaze technique, tiles are painted first and then dipped into liquid and fired. The glaze is transparent and shows the design through it.

Coloured glaze and underglaze are used mainly for polychrome tiles. The third technique, overglaze painting, is monochrome ceramic with opaque coloured glaze painted over and fired.

The art of ceramic revetment reached its height under Timur and his descendants in fifteenth-century Central Asia. Even after the collapse of the Timurid empire the faience mosaic and blue tiles that were its hallmark continued to exert strong influence on later flowerings of ceramic art in Iran and Turkey. The Tiled Pavilion, built in the gardens of Topkapi Palace in Istanbul in 1472, for example, shows strong Timurid influence in its architectural concept and decoration.

Post-Timurid Bukhara

In Central Asia, the Uzbeks slavishly copied Timurid art, but political instability and loss of the Silk Roads trade led to economic depression and cultural decline. With the passing of the Shaibanid dynasty at the end of the sixteenth century, the Uzbek empire split into three squabbling Khanates of Khiva, Bukhara – including Samarkand – and Kokand.

Insignificant and increasingly isolated from the rest of the world, the Khanates were unable to maintain the earlier fine cultural traditions of Central Asia. Samarkand, indeed, was virtually uninhabited from the 1720s to the 1770s, although Bukhara continued to benefit from the pilgrim trade and some architecturally interesting buildings were put up.

Reached through a maze of narrow twisting streets, the Char Minar, or Four Minarets, is a most unusual building of this later period. This strange little structure with four bulbous minarets dwarfing a central dome, was originally built in 1807 by a rich Bukhariot merchant as the gate-house to a madrasa which has since disappeared.

Even later, Uzbek architecture seemingly rebelled against centuries of massive, monumental structure; or, some say, the builders simply economized because of the region's declining fortunes. But, whatever the reason, slender wooden pillars replaced sturdy mud-brick arches, fragile open fronts superceded solid portals, and even domes disappeared.

One of the best examples of this new delicate style is the Masjid-i-Jami built beside the pleasant Bola Hauz across the Registan from the Ark. This mosque is open-fronted and deeply recessed, the recess forming a shelter for worshippers. Only a carved wooden trellis separates it from the street, and the roof is supported by 20 slender wooden pillars with carved capitals. The inside walls are tiled and the ceiling is painted a multitude of designs in a rainbow of colours.

Nothing in Bukhara compares, however, with the riot of styles and colours incorporated into Sitora-i-Makhi Khasa, the suburban residence of the last Bukhara amirs. Its garish green, blue, red and orange ceramic-coated portal are an insult to the tiles of the Timurid period, and its Uzbek baroque interior a mockery of the purity of earlier Central Asian decor. For a dynasty isolated from the rest of the world and increasingly threatened by Russia, this building represented a final desperate last fling.

Although the façade of Mir-i-Arab has lost most of its ceramic facing, the college's beautifully proportioned twin domes – characteristically covered with blue tiles and ringed by an elegant band of calligraphic script – have been carefully restored.

Above Characteristics of Bukhara's search for cool and shade, fountains play brightly on Bola Hauz, while in the background stands Masjid-i-Jami mosque with its deeply recessed front forming a shelter from the sun for worshippers.

Left The carved stalactite capitol of one of the 20 wooden pillars supporting the recessed roof of Masjid-i-Jami mosque. Characteristically, Central Asian architects made thrifty use of scarce wood and sought to make the most of its decorative qualities.

Above left A detail from the riot of styles and colours found at Sitora-i-Makhi Khasa.

Above right The baroque interior of Sitora-i-Makhi Khasa, the final playground of the Bukhara amirs before they were ousted by the Red Army.

Below By comparison with the majestic portals and ceramic decor of the Timurid and early Uzbek periods, this puny, garish gateway to Sitora-i-Makhi Khasa, the suburban residence of the last Bukhara amirs, is a low point in Central Asian architecture.

4 Glasnost and Samarkand

For centuries, Samarkand and Bukhara, the once-great cities of the Golden Road, preserved only the romance of their names and the vague memory that, long ago, they had somehow been important. Nonetheless, the brilliant artistic legacy of the Timurids – in calligraphy, poetry, metalwork, bookbinding and a broad range of other arts, as well as architecture – did survive, and in careful restorations now under way in the Soviet Union, as well as in museum exhibitions in Europe and the United States, it is receiving the recognition it deserves.

Simultaneously, the policies of *perestroika* (economic restructuring) and *glasnost* (openness) ushered in by Mikhail Gorbachev during the 1980s are not only making it possible for foreigners to visit central Asia easily for the first time, but, more importantly, are allowing the people who live there to re-establish the kind of international contacts the region has been denied since the demise of the Silk Roads.

In 1990 an international competition was launched among architects around the world to select the best ideas for revitalizing the historic core of Samarkand. The first step will be to build a multi-purpose cultural complex, named after the astronomer Ulugh Beg, that will provide for entertainment, festivals and folk dances, business and commercial opportunities, cultural pursuits and international conferences. In addition, sports and recreational activities, exhibitions and religious ceremonies will be held within the centre.

The competition, sponsored by the architects' unions of the Soviet Union and Uzbekistan and the Aga Khan Trust for Culture, aims to resolve two critical problems facing Samarkand today: how to integrate a complex of contemporary buildings in the midst of a historical city and in the immediate proximity of some of the world's most beautiful and significant monuments; and how to provide a cultural centre that will become not only the focus of the city, but also an important catalyst for the emerging cultural identity of the citizens of Samarkand.

For, although we tend to think of the inhabitants of the Union of Soviet Socialist Republics as simply Russians, there are over one hundred non-Russian nationalities living in the USSR. And, after a century of near-invisibility to the casual observer, they are making their presence felt in today's changing Soviet Union. Of the Union's 15 republics, 6 – including Uzbekistan – are still, despite decades of religious repression, consciously Muslim. In fact, the Soviet Union's 53

The glazed tiles, with which medieval Central Asian architects sheathed such buildings as Shirdar Madrasa in Samarkand, enabled the defining of outlines required to create geometric patterns and served excellently in Islamic non-representational decoration of walls and domes.

million Muslims compose almost one-fifth of the entire 280 million population of the USSR. After ethnic Russians, they are its second-largest population group. And since their numbers are growing four times as fast as the Soviet population as a whole, Soviet Muslims are projected to outnumber Russians in 30 years.

Of these Muslims, the Uzbeks, who number about 20 million, are the largest nationality, and because they have remained settled for the longer period of time, they have the strongest cultural and religious traditions. The other Muslims are also mainly Turkic: Azaris, Balkars, Bashkirs, Karachays, Karakalpaks, Kazaks, Kirgiz, Kumyks, Tatars and Turkmen. Along with the Farsi-speaking Tajiks, they occupy the vast crescent of land stretching from Europe to China along the southern rim of the USSR. All these peoples, descendants of the fierce nomad tribes of Mongolia and one-time rulers of Central Asia, were swallowed up in the south-easterly expansion of Russia's czarist empire in the nineteenth century. In 1927, the Soviets – successors of the Russian empire after the communist revolution of 1917 – divided their Central Asian dominions into six republics, naming them after the majority Muslim nationalities that lived there: Azerbaijan, Kazakstan, Kirgizia, Tajikstan, Turkmenia and Uzbekistan.

Modern Uzbekistan

Uzbekistan, with its ancient cities of Samarkand, Bukhara, Khiva and Kokand, is the heir to Central Asia's glorious past. Lying between the Aral Sea in the north and Afganistan in the south, it covers some 449,600 sq km (173,600 sq miles). The north-western half of Uzbekistan is largely desert, while the south-eastern half includes the great fertile valleys of Ferghana and Zeravshan.

In 1928, after Stalin came to power, the wholesale closure – and in many cases destruction – of mosques began throughout Soviet Central Asia. In a campaign that continued until World War II, the communists shut down or destroyed all but 400 of Central Asia's 26,000 mosques and all but two of its religious colleges – the Mir-i-Arab Madrasa in Bukhara and the Tashkent Institute. Muslims, however, managed to keep their religion alive by their own grass-roots efforts: through hundreds of illegal Koranic schools and unofficial prayer centres, and through the work and faith of thousands of itinerant, unofficial clerics.

After years of attempting to eradicate Islam, the Soviets, under

Coloured and patterned to form larger designs, like these at Khiva, tiles were used by Muslim architects to cover continuous surfaces, and, in Central Asia, became an indispensible element of Islamic architecture.

Left Since the relaxation of religious restrictions in the USSR under Mikhail Gorbachev, the sanctuary of Bagaut Din, near Bukhara, has once more become a place of popular pilgrimage. A complex of small mosques, courtyards and shrines, the sanctuary's free-standing minaret is a mini-version of Bukhara's giant Kalyan Tower.

Overleaf Before the Soviet authorities removed the population in order to rebuild ancient Khiva, this desolate expanse dominated by a deserted madrasa was the city's bustling central square.

Gorbachev, are allowing more religious freedom and are relaxing previously rigid controls on mosque permits. In Samarkand, for instance, there are now 23 functioning mosques compared to only three two years ago, and in Bukhara the Mir-i-Arab Madrasa has been given permission to increase its number of students from 80 to 200. There are thousands of mosques, all with historical significance, still standing in Central Asia, and the Muslim clergy are hoping that many of these too will soon be open for worship.

Although not yet functioning as a mosque, the Kalyan Mosque in Bukhara has already been handed over to the religious authorities, and the suburban shrine of Bagaut Din has once more become a place of popular pilgrimage. Some days hundreds can be seen filing through the religious complex to pray beneath a mulberry tree by the saint's well-kept tomb.

For while ruthlessly trying to eradicate Islam in the present, the Soviet authorities have taken great care to preserve as monuments important vestiges of its past, especially in Uzbekistan whose 8 million rouble annual subsidy from Moscow to maintain historical buildings is the largest of any of the union's 15 republics. Although, with a total of 11,000 monuments in Uzbekistan, officials say 50 to 60 million are needed to do a proper job.

These officials are pressing Intourist, the government organization which handles all foreign travel within the Soviet Union, to give part of its earnings to preserve ancient monuments. 'Without the monuments there would be no tourism,' says Faruz Ashrafi, head of Uzbekistan's Council for Conservation and Preservation of Monuments and Culture. He wants Intourist to hand over 25 per cent of its profits from tourism in the republic to his organization.

Many Uzbeks are angry about the economic relationship between their republic and Moscow. Uzbekistan produces 67 per cent of the cotton grown in the Soviet Union. But according to Rafik Nishanov, a former first secretary of the Central Committee of the Communist Party of Uzbekistan, only 6 per cent of the cotton grown in Uzbekistan is processed and sold there. The rest is sent to the Russian Socialist Federal Soviet Republic – Russia proper – for processing, and most of the products made from it are sold abroad to earn hard currency.

The people of Uzbekistan are also angry with Moscow for what it has done to the Aral Sea, which forms part of the republic's northern

border. Once the world's fourth largest lake, the Aral has shrunk by 50 per cent because state economic planners diverted water from its two feeder rivers – the Amu Darya and the Syr Darya – in order to irrigate fields to grow still more cotton. What little water reaches the Aral and its deltas is a soup of fertilizers and pesticides.

Some 30,000 sq km (10,000 sq miles) of former lake bed now lie exposed as a desert of salt and chemicals which, blown across the republic, has precipitated a public health disaster. Infant mortality is high, and throat cancer, hepatitis and stomach disorders are endemic.

Moscow's craving for cotton is also destroying the 'veritable Garden of Eden' that Lord Curzon found in the 1880s in the Zeravshan valley. 'Until the cotton is planted right up to the patio outside your window, what must be done,' asked the Uzbek writer Hashimov recently. 'Where are we going to get meat, milk and butter?'

Constant irrigation of the cotton fields has also caused the water table to rise in the Samarkand and Bukhara oases, reaching the foundations of many ancient monuments. The fertilizer-saturated water is soaked up by their walls and pillars, then evaporates through their surfaces leaving behind chemicals that eat into the structure. Salt crystallized behind paintwork and gilding also eventually pushes them off the walls.

This problem is clearly evident in the recently restored mosque of Tilakar Madrasa in Samarkand's Registan, where, despite drill holes in the walls to facilitate evaporation, paintwork is already beginning to peel.

Preservation versus Reconstruction

Discussion of these problems has only been possible since *glasnost*, a new openness which has unleashed a heated debate among architects and builders on whether it is proper to reconstruct ancient monuments as they once were, or better to preserve them as they now stand. So far, the former policy has prevailed. But now the latter is gaining ground. Certainly one of the most dramatic monuments in Central Asia is the colossal ruined arch of Timur's White Palace, Akserai, at Shahrisabz, while the rebuilt old city of Khiva leaves most people cold.

Khiva, which became the capital of the Khorezm oasis after Urgench was destroyed by Genghiz Khan in 1219 in revenge for the execution of his envoy by the Khorezmshahs, was until recently one of the most colourful old cities in Central Asia. Indeed, a British captain named

Left A pristine mud-brick wall and as-new minaret characteristic of Khiva's rebuilt 'ancient' monuments.

Right This carved marble base and wooden pillar at Khiva, is original, not a modern copy.

Buraby who journeyed there in 1876 recommended that 'should the Russian Government ever permit Englishmen to travel in their Asiatic dominions', Khiva should be included by 'Mr. Cook on the list of his personally conducted tours'.

The Soviets, with tourism in mind, have made Khiva a 'town preserve' – all its inhabitants, with the exception of about 2,000, have been moved out of the old walled city into the adjoining new town, and its ancient buildings have been rebuilt or restored. The walls surrounding the old city – wide at the bottom, tapering up to about 2 m (6 ft) at the top – have also been rebuilt and carefully replastered with mud.

There is hardly a cracked tile in the colourful bands of different patterned ceramics which ring the city's two main minarets from top to bottom: the squat nineteenth-century Unfinished Minaret, so called because it only reached half its original height; and the Islam Hodja Minaret, built at the beginning of this century, which towers to a height of 50 m (166 ft). The latter offers a bird's eye view of the yellow-grey domes of the mainly nineteenth-century mosques and madrasas that sprawl around the Tash-Khauli Palace, the residence of the last khans of Khiva. It boasts 160 rooms, adorned with over 100 differently designed tile coverings and carved plasterwork, known as 'ganche', and a maze of courtyards whose cloisters and verandas are supported by elegant wooden columns on carved marble bases.

Today Khiva's maze of narrow streets are probably the cleanest in Central Asia, its strong fortress walls the most upright, its portals and cupolas least damaged and its turrets and minarets the most straight. But *is* it right to sneer 'Disneyland'? Soviet archaeologists are confident about their knowledge of Khiva's ancient buildings, which are not that old, and the craftsmen employed to rebuild them have done an excellent job. But it *is* a replica, and it has no soul.

Better go to Shahrisabz with Don de Clavijo in your pocket and stand beneath the crumbling arch of Akserai and imagine it as it all was. According to Don de Clavijo, who visited Shahrisabz on his way to Samarkand, Akserai stood in a courtyard 271 m (900 ft) wide, paved with white flagstones and surrounded by an arcade. In the centre was a large pool, before which rose the palace itself, with its great central arch entrance, at least 50 m (165 ft) high and with a span of about 22 m (74 ft). This central gateway was covered with gold and blue tiles and

Above Craftsmen repainting the ceiling of the boudoir of one of the Khiva Khan's wives at Tash-Khauli Palace.

Below Hazrati Hizr Mosque, overlooking a main highway at Samarkand, was once crowded with caravan travellers praying, or giving thanks, for a safe journey. Today, however, only a few tourists disturb its dozing guardian to pay their admission fees.

Now just a gaunt ruin, Timur's White Palace at Shahrisabz, has outlived the empires of the Timurids, the Uzbeks and the Russian czars. And although Lenin still strikes a defiant pose in the adjacent square, the palace could outlive communism too. Even in decay, the tilework adorning the two giant fragments *(right)* is a tribute to fifteenth-century ceramists.

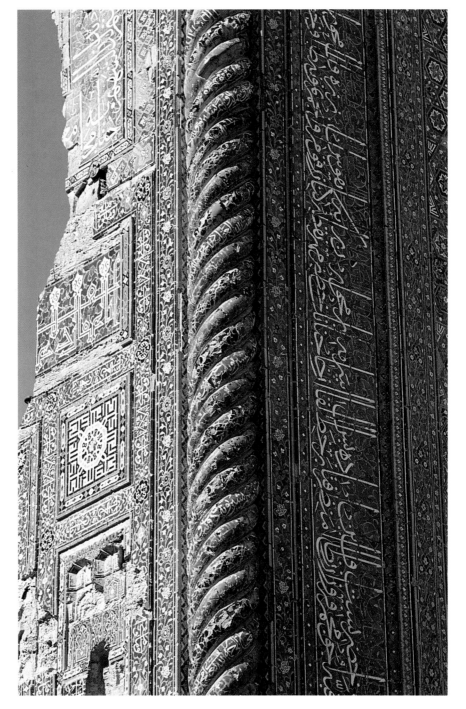

surmounted, as were two other smaller arches – one either side – by figures of the lion and the sun. Through the central arch lay a large reception hall, a square-domed room whose walls were panelled with tiles and whose ceiling was gilded. Beyond this was a banqueting hall, 'very spacious and gorgeously adorned'.

> We were taken into galleries and in these likewise everywhere the walls were of gilt tiles,' wrote de Clavijo. 'We saw indeed here so many apartments and separate chambers, all of which were adorned with tile-work of blue and gold with many other colours, and all was so marvellously wrought that even the craftsmen of Paris, so noted for their skill, would hold that which is done here to be very fine workmanship.

Of Timur's great palace, only two gigantic fragments of the piers of the entrance portal still stand; but the tilework, even in its decay, is magnificent.

Valeri Lavrenko, who heads Bukhara's conservation efforts, believes: 'It is better to preserve than reconstruct, because although we know the secrets of the old masters, we do not have the same materials to work with'. In fact, wherever possible in Bukhara, original materials are cleaned and re-used in restoring old buildings, rather than using new ones.

In Samarkand, where, according to the official guide book 'history comes face to face with socialist realism', there is an obvious clash of ideals. 'There is a conflict of interest between the need to build more flats and houses and to preserve the old city', says Raisa Pavlovna Torasenko, deputy head of municipal planning.

So far, the developers seem to have had the upper hand.

Samarkand's former chief architect Nematjan Sadikov drew up plans for traditional housing to replace the slums torn down around the Registan. But pressure from local Communist Party officials led instead to the construction of five-storey blocks of flats. Sadikov, however, remains optimistic: 'Seventy years (under Communism) is *nothing* in the history of Samarkand. Because of what is happening in the Soviet Union, things could change'.

Above Workmen rebuilding the arches surrounding the courtyard of Bukhara's Kalyan Mosque. Once the city's largest mosque it has been handed back to the religious authorities and could soon begin functioning again as a place of worship.

Below Although the three monumental madrasas flanking Samarkand's Registan have been restored to their former splendour, they still need constant attention from conservationists.

Overleaf A good omen for Central Asia and its people: a stork's nest – a traditional sign of good luck – sits atop the dome of Bukhara's Kalyan Mosque.

Travellers' Information

Planning the trip

Getting There

Although the Soviet Union is not yet fully geared to individual travel, *Glasnost* is changing things fast. Private travel agencies are sprouting up throughout the Soviet Union to challenge the monopolistic State tourist organization, Intourist. On-the-spot visas – although expensive at £50 for three days – are now available at Moscow airport. And the enforced guided tour of a factory or communal farm is a thing of the past.

It remains virtually impossible, however, to book hotels direct and, in the short term at least, the cheapest and most convenient way of visiting Samarkand or Bukhara is as part of a group tour including other Soviet cities.

Intourist offers a fourteen day tour of the Soviet Union, including two days each in Samarkand and Bukhara, at prices ranging from £665 to £869 per person, sharing a twin-bedded room. Other cities included in the itinerary are Moscow (where you have to stay overnight in any case to get almost anywhere in the USSR), Leningrad and Tashkent, the modern capital of Uzbekistan. Included in the price are return airfare London-Moscow, all internal travel, half-board (bed and breakfast and dinner) and excursions. Because single rooms are rare in the Soviet Union, they cost £25 a day extra.

Intourist also offers 'à la carte' tours which you can make up from a menu of twenty cities, but dawdling in Samarkand and Bukhara, where accommodation is limited, is discouraged. Officially, the maximum stay in Samarkand is three nights and Bukhara two, but like everything else in the Soviet Union, this is loosening up.

Intourist has offices in most western capitals – in Britain it has branches in London (071-538 8600), Manchester (061-834 0230) and Glasgow (041-204 1402) – and offers the widest range of tours in the Soviet Union.

Leading British tour operators, including Thomas Cook (0800-881234), Thompson Worldwide (071-387 8484) and Voyages Jules Verne (071-486 8000), also offer a limited range of package tours, but tend to shy away from arranging individual travel; and when they do, it is expensive.

One agency willing to organize individual itineraries at reasonable cost is Progressive Tours (071-262 1676). For 1991 they were quoting £360 for airfares London-Moscow-Samarkand-Bukhara return, £50 per person per night bed and breakfast in Samarkand and Bukhara, and £80 to £90 for the necessary overnight stay in Moscow (there are no direct international flights or same-day connections to and from Central Asia). If you do not want to see anything of Moscow, an overnight stay at the internal Sheremetevo Airport costs 50 roubles (£5). Rail travel to Samarkand and Bukhara from Moscow costs £65 one way – only £5 less than the air fare – and takes two days.

Allow at least two months to make individual travel arrangements, and do not be too disappointed if you do not get exactly what you want. On receipt of payment you will be given a wad of vouchers for each service booked, which you hand in at the hotel or local Intourist office in exchange for rooms, air tickets, etc.

Travel documents

All Western visitors to the Soviet Union need visas. You can apply direct to the nearest Soviet Consulate (in London: 5 Kensington Palace Gardens, W8; tel: 071-229 6412) with a letter from your Travel Agency and confirmation of your hotel reservations and transport bookings. To avoid long queues, let your travel agent handle your visas application for a £3-£10 fee. If you are booked on a package tour, the agent will automatically handle visas.

An immunisation certificate is not required by Westerners visiting the Soviet Union. But although health hazards have been greatly reduced in recent decades in Central Asia, it is wise to drink bottled water and beware of unwashed fruit and salads. Carry basic medicines, which are not always readily available in the USSR.

Climate

Situated in the middle of the Eurasian landmass, far from an ocean, Samarkand and Bukahra have hot, dry climates with temperatures ranging from minus 15 to minus 20 centigrade in January to plus 42 to 47 centigrade in July. The best time to visit is between these extremes, in spring or autumn.

Currency

The recent massive devaluation of the rouble affects local hard currency exchanges only. And although, at ten roubles to the pound sterling, this makes on-the-spot rouble purchase ridiculously cheap, you will still have to pay for most of your trip (including all advance arrangements for hotels, transport and meals) in hard currency at the old rate of one rouble to the pound sterling. Goods bought at hotel shops, drinks in hotel bars and excursions arranged by local Intourist offices are also payable in hard currency.

Staying in Samarkand and Bukhara

Eating
The Soviet Union's recurring food shortages, together with the nomadic ancestry of the Uzbeks, is reflected in the limited choice – mostly lamb-based stews and kebabs – of hotel fare. Restaurants offer even less, if anything at all. The best way to supplement this monotonous menu is to stock up on readily available fresh fruits at local markets or search out an open-air food stall, where at least the kebabs are charcoal grilled and the bread fresh. One such establishment is located opposite the entrace of Ulugh Beg Observatory in Samarkand, and several are situated around Bukhara's Holy Pool. Both have tables and chairs where you can eat your food.

Shopping
Although there are few handicrafts to buy – even the famous Bukhara carpets are now machine made and all exported – manufactured Bukhara silks, embroidered Uzbek skull caps and sequined slippers can be bought in hotel shops and some bazaars. You may even find women in the bazaars selling some of their own antique jewellery or small hand-made carpets, or a man with a pair of real leather, knee-high boots. Travellers' cheques are accepted, as are leading credit cards, in most shops dealing in hard currency. Bazaars are strictly cash.

Sightseeing
Read up as much as you can before you go. Local guide books in English, with the exception of the hard to find one about Samarkand, are non-existent. Local English-speaking guides, however, are informative and available through Intourist. A car and driver can also be hired through Intourist, which has offices in most hotels. Intourist can also arrange out-of-town excursions, such as from Samarkand to Shahrisabz. All these services are payable in hard currency. Cruising taxis are cheap, but hard to find. A small charge is made for entrance to most monuments.

Communications
Forget the rest of the world and enjoy Central Asia, which, by modern standards, is still somewhat cut off. Foreign language newspapers are rare and out of date. International telephone calls must be booked at least two days in advance (use telegrams in an emergency, which are fast), and postcards will probably arrive home before you do.

Further Reading

Golden Road to Samarkand, Wilfred Blunt, Hamish Hamilton, 1987

To the Back and Beyond: An Illustrated Companion to Central Asia, Maclean Fitzroy, A. Case, 1974

Central Asia, Gavin Hambly, Weidenfeld, 1969

The Cambridge History of Early Inner Asia, Denis Sinor, Cambridge University Press, 1990

Russia in Central Asia, Lord Curzon, Longmans, 1889

Setting the East Ablaze: Lenin's Dream of an Empire in Central Asia, Peter Hopkirk, John Murray, 1984

Imperial Nomads: A History of Central Asia, Luc Kwaten, Leicester University Press, 1979

Through Khiva to Golden Samarkand, Ella R. Christie, Seely, Service & Co., 1925

Index